Treasure in Heaven

RICHARD LECTURES FOR 2012

TREASURE IN HEAVEN

The Holy Poor in Early Christianity

PETER BROWN

University of Virginia Press

CHARLOTTESVILLE AND LONDON

University of Virginia Press
© 2016 by the Rector and Visitors of the University of Virginia
All rights reserved
Printed in the United States of America on acid-free paper

First published 2016

9 8 7 6 5 4 3 2 1

LIBRARY OF CONGRESS CATALOGING-IN-PUBLICATION DATA
Brown, Peter, 1935–
 Treasure in heaven : the holy poor in early Christianity / Peter Brown.
  pages   cm.—(Richard lectures for 2012)
 Includes bibliographical references and index.
  ISBN 978-0-8139-3828-8 (cloth : alk. paper)—ISBN 978-0-8139-3829-5
(e-book)
  1. Poverty—Religious aspects—Christianity. 2. Church work with
the poor. 3. Church history—Primitive and early church, ca. 30–600.
4. Middle East—Church history. I. Title.
 BR195.P68B76 2016
 270.1—dc23

2015017651

For Betsy

Contents

Acknowledgments

This book is based on the James W. Richard Lectures which I delivered at the University of Virginia in November 2012. It was an occasion of great happiness and of considerable intellectual profit for me. I have warm memories of the enthusiasm and kindness of Professor Mark Whittle, the chair of the Page-Barbour and James W. Richard Lectures Committee, and of a gathering of scholars from all disciplines (faculty and graduate students alike) who made the welcome extended to me joyous and memorable. For a series of magical days, the words of the old Latin tag *Ubi amici ibi patria*—where there are friends, there is one's homeland—came true. And to claim the University of Virginia as one's *patria*—one's home campus—if only for a week, is an occasion for pride. I was honored to take part in the life of such a remarkable and resilient academic community.

In the process of turning these lectures into a book, I realized how much I owed to younger scholars who have ventured deeper than I have into fields that have only recently been opened up to scholars of late antiquity. In matters Syriac, I owe a particular debt to David Michelson and to Jack Tannous; in matters Coptic, to Ariel López. Anne-Marie Luijendijk and Derek Krueger looked at earlier drafts with insight and with characteristic generosity.

From beginning to end, my wife, Betsy, brought to every draft and every detail of this manuscript her alert eye for imprecisions and infelicities of style. But above all she brought a zest for wider worlds and for ever more searching explanations that has characterized our friendship over so many years. It is only appropriate that I should dedicate this book to her on the twenty-fifth anniversary of our marriage.

Introduction

From the Real to the Holy Poor

This book began as the James W. Richard Lectures delivered at the University of Virginia in November 2012. The lectures dealt with the nature of religious giving in early Christianity from the time of Saint Paul to the rise of monasticism in the fourth and fifth centuries AD.

They arose from a sense of discovery. For at least ten years I had been studying the use of wealth and the relations between rich and poor in the Christianity of the late antique period.[1] When I began my studies, in around 2000, I thought that I knew who the "poor" were, and what was considered to be the proper relations between rich and poor in Christian communities. I assumed that every Christian (and especially every rich Christian) was expected to spend a portion of his or her wealth on the support of the poor, through the giving of alms. This practice was based on the clear words of Jesus Christ: *"give to the poor, and then thou shalt have treasure in heaven"* (Matt. 19:21).

I wrote my two books on this topic—*Poverty and Leadership* and *Through the Eye of a Needle*—between 2000 and 2012. In them, I concentrated on the extent to which the rich lived up to the challenge of Christ. I also studied the institutions that were developed for the care of the poor, and the circumstances that led to charitable ventures within the Christian communities. Finally, I considered what problems (practical and ideological) were raised in late Roman society as a whole by the novel Christian emphasis on almsgiving to the poor.

But while I was writing these books, I began to reflect on another, less obvious theme. As I read further in other Christian sources and in the history of other, non-Christian regions (I think particularly of the sociology of Buddhism),[2] I became increasingly aware of the importance of a further category of the poor—the "holy" poor. These were persons who received alms and other forms of support, not because they were "poor" in the economic sense, but because they were "poor" in a more intangible, religious sense. They had abandoned their usual means of support so as to pursue the highest aims of the Christian life. They no longer worked. Instead they looked to others to support them. In many cases, they were as dependent on the labor and gifts of pious Christians as were any beggars.

The "holy poor" had a long history. They were there in the time of Saint Paul. Not only did Paul make collections to support *the poor among the saints in Jerusalem* (Rom. 15:26). But he also argued fiercely about the degree to which "apostles" and other leaders (such as himself) might claim support from the local Christian communities.

Paul's letters were inconclusive on these matters. They left all succeeding generations of Christians with an unresolved dilemma. On the one hand, Paul was believed by later Christians to have laid down a strict rule for the Christian community at Thessalonica: *"If any one will not work, let him not eat"* (2 Thess. 3:10). On the other hand, Paul himself had hinted in other letters that there were some special believers whose high degree of religious commitment entitled them to be fed from the work of others. As he wrote to the Christians of Corinth: *"If we have sown spiritual good among you, is it too much to reap your material support?"* (1 Cor. 9:11).

In modern times, New Testament scholars have claimed to have resolved this dilemma. They assert that the Second Letter to the Thessalonians was not written by Paul, but by disciples of Paul, anxious to clear up an ambiguity that their master had failed to address. The early Christians who form the subject of this book, however, enjoyed no such easy way out. For them Paul was, in no uncertain manner, *Saint* Paul. Every letter ascribed to him in the New Testament was his own. It reflected his own, distinctive mind, wrestling to communicate a single, apostolic message. And on the issue of labor and the "holy poor" Paul seemed to have spoken with two voices. It was for good Christians to try to reconcile these voices. Like the intricate music of a fugue (or the seemingly endless interweaving of patterns on a modern computer screen), the permutations of the two voices of Paul—the Paul who claimed material support for his high venture and the Paul of the Second Letter to the Thessalonians—wove in and out in the writings of all Christians from one end of this book to the other. Far from being resolved, the tensions set up by the words ascribed to Saint Paul were as challenging to the religious imagination in the fifth century as they had been in the first.

Indeed, the "holy poor" (as they came to be called) were still there, and in ever-larger numbers, four centuries after the days of Paul, in the fourth and fifth centuries AD. By that time the monastic movement in the eastern provinces of the Roman Empire had filled the landscape with holy figures, many of whom (though not all) had abandoned work in favor of a life of contemplation and prayer on behalf of others. Institutions such as monasteries and convents had arisen, some of whose members claimed proudly to be self-supporting, while others were equally proud to be supported entirely by the gifts of the faithful.

In between the days of Paul and the rise of monasticism—that is, in the second and third centuries AD—the Christian church set down firm roots in Roman society largely because its bishops and clergy, also, claimed to be members of the "holy poor." Like the "holy poor," they expected to be freed from normal work (either fully or in part) through the support of the faithful. This support enabled them to pursue full-time ecclesiastical careers as preachers, teachers, and as administrators of the wealth of the church on behalf of the "real" poor. What we call the "professionalization" of the clergy rested on the decision to treat the clergy as a special kind of poor, supported (like the poor) by the free-will offerings of the faithful.

These "holy poor" were not what we call "the deserving poor"—the poor who were deemed to qualify for support because, though poor, they were not shiftless. Christians (like Jews) frequently winnowed the ranks of the poor to distinguish between the deserving poor and work-shy, fraudulent beggars. But the "holy poor" belonged to an entirely different category. They had, of course, to establish their claims to support. As we shall see, from the time of Saint Paul onward, these claims were often hotly contested. But once accepted, members of the "holy poor" were thought to have a numinous quality about them. Men and women alike, they were treated by their fellow Christians as persons who received material support in exchange for offering immeasurable immaterial benefits—teaching, preaching, and prayer. They were an elite. To support them—quite as much as to support the "real" poor—was to place *treasure in heaven*.

As a result, the category of the "holy poor" raised an acute problem for the religious imagination. They were inevitably more prominent than were the "real" poor. They stood out as mediators between the average believers and God. Gifts to them were thought to bring salvation and blessing in ways that always seemed more direct and more palpable than the equally mysterious, but somehow more shadowy, less easily focused reward of *treasure in heaven* promised to those who gave alms to the real poor. The real poor lacked faces as the holy poor did not.

It was not in any way surprising for a religious movement to throw up a prominent class of *virtuosi* and administrators, whose members claimed to be entitled to special support. What was distinctive about the Christianity of this period was the manner in which the claims of the holy poor pushed to the fore an explosive issue that affected Roman society as a whole—the issue of work.

Support of the holy poor cast a shadow of doubt on one of the building blocks of Roman society—on labor itself. To what extent was labor to be regarded as an inescapable part of the human condition? Or was labor no more than a sad side effect of the fall of humanity? Was it the result of some abrupt decline from an age of abundance and carefree leisure into a world of toil? If that was so, was it possible to reverse the fallen state of a humanity condemned to toil, in order to set free a privileged few, who could rise to higher things through being supported by the labor of others?

This was no abstract issue. In the ancient world, leisure—freedom from labor—had been the jealously guarded privilege of the elites. From the first century onward, these elites found themselves confronted by a Christian movement that, in the name of religion, set free an entire category of persons who, in normal conditions, would have been tied to the drudgery of work. These work-free persons were disturbingly active. They would build communities; they would preach; they would roam the roads; they would bring the blessings of teaching, prayer, and healing to thousands. As the "holy poor," they were enabled to do this because they had been freed from labor by contributions provided by the majority of their fellow believers, for whom work remained an unavoidable necessity.

As a result, debates on the role of work in human society exploded with a vehemence, tenacity, and sophistication that increasingly came to fascinate me. Here we could listen to the subdued groan of an entire society caught in the toils of labor. It was a theme which could be followed from the very beginnings of civilization in the ancient Near East to the last centuries of the Roman Empire. It took me from the myths and wisdom literature of ancient Mesopotamia, in the third and second millennia BC, through the *Works and Days* of Hesiod, to the exegesis of the story of the fall of Adam and Eve from the garden of Eden (recorded in the first chapters of the book of Genesis), as this was expounded by Syrian ascetics in the fifth century AD.

Altogether, I found myself confronted with a theme that ran from one end of the history of the Christian church to the other, joining the ages in a common tension: how much of the wealth of Christians should go to support the real poor and how much should go to the "holy poor"? As I read further, I increasingly realized that the historical study of the finances and of the social impact of the Christian church had tended to concentrate largely on the care of the "real" poor. A lively tradition of scholarship, from which I have learned much, has already begun to do justice to that particular challenge: poverty, almsgiving, and the notion of the poor in Christian circles have been extremely well studied by young scholars in the past decade.[3] But a complete study of the Christian use of wealth in late antiquity must also include the demands made by a further, vivid segment of the Christian community—the "holy poor." Like the swirling currents of a great river, the two streams (the "real" poor and the "holy" poor) intermingled, throughout the centuries, in all debates on religious giving in Christian circles.

Toward the East: A *Greek* Roman Empire

In pursuing this theme, I found that I had returned to a region of the Roman world on which I had not concentrated for some time. In the last decade, my work on wealth and poverty had concentrated largely on the Latin West. My large book, *Through the Eye of a Needle*, and my subsequent short book, *The Ransom of the Soul*, dealt largely with Latin Christianity.[4] In terms of geographical focus these two books overlap in no way with the present book. In this book, I have moved to the East. I have found myself in what is usually called "the Greek East." The term "Greek East" is no more than a facilitating simplification. (As we will see, one of the characteristics of the late Roman period was the emergence of non-Greek languages and cultural traditions in major regions of the Roman East.) But it is a simplification that helps us to make a clear distinction between the eastern parts of the Roman Empire, where (with some significant exceptions) Greek was the dominant language of government and culture, and the Latin-speaking world of the West.

In late antiquity, East and West emerged, effectively, as two different worlds. The pace of change in the one was very different from the pace of change in the other. In western Europe, the Roman Empire declined and fell. The story of the fall of the empire in the West was the "awful revolution" on which Edward Gibbon concentrated in his *History of the Decline and Fall of the Roman Empire*.[5] But the more we study the eastern provinces of the Roman Empire, the more we realize that the "awful revolution" described by Gibbon was an event restricted to western Europe. And, at that time, western Europe was not the center of the world. Seen from the East, the fall of Rome in the West took place in a distant, northwestern corner of the vast landmass of Eurasia. The unraveling of empire that happened there did not greatly affect the ancient heartlands of civilization. These were still securely established in the eastern Mediterranean and in the Middle East. In those regions, the "awful revolution," to which western Europeans have devoted so much melancholy attention, did not happen.

What mattered, in the Greek East, was the late Roman revolution in government that created, in the eastern provinces of the Roman world, a remarkably stable imperial system. This imperial system stretched from the Balkans to the Caucasus and as far south as the cataracts of Egypt. It would last until the Arab invasions of the seventh century. At a time when the Roman provinces of the West had entered a postimperial stage, under barbarian rule, the eastern provinces of the empire enjoyed a *pax Byzantina*—a "Byzantine," east Roman peace—that was as secure, as buoyed up by economic expansion, and seemingly as unchanging as the *pax Romana* had once been in the age of Marcus Aurelius.

Altogether, a Roman Empire that was still somewhat insecure in its control of the eastern provinces in the time of Saint Paul was still there, expanded and solidified, almost four hundred years later, when Symeon Stylites, the great Christian hermit, mounted his column within full view of the ancient Roman road—parts of which have still survived—that led from Antioch to the Persian frontier. In terms of the imperial framework in which the events that I describe in this book took place, time had stood still.

But this was not the case with east Roman society itself. East Roman society evolved rapidly and with increasing confidence to create a world very different from that of classical times. After the severe crisis caused by civil war and barbarian invasion in the third century, the empire rallied definitively in the East. The foundation of Constantinople in 324 by Constantine the Great (306–37) was the most enduring sign of this rallying. Constantinople (modern Istanbul, Turkey) was very much "Constantine's City"—*Konstantinou Polis*. It was intended to register the opening of a new age, associated with the person of the first Christian emperor. But the foundation of Constantinople turned out to be more than an imperial ego trip. The establishment of a major city at the point where the roads from Europe crossed into Asia, and the Black Sea flowed into the Mediterranean, validated a silent and irreversible revolution. The center of gravity of the Roman world had shifted toward the East. Constantinople was called "the New Rome." It was a Rome brought close to home for the inhabitants of the eastern provinces. Very soon, for these inhabitants, old Rome dropped from view. The only Rome they knew, or needed to know, was the New Rome of Constantine and his eastern successors.[6]

Those of us who turn our attention to the East are now confronted by exciting new developments. Through the patient work of archaeologists all over the eastern Mediterranean and the Middle East, we have learned that many of the regions of the empire of "New Rome" were characterized by marked agrarian growth and by increased commercial interchange. In particular, the landscapes across which the Christian monastic movement exploded, in Egypt and Syria, have been revealed to have been thriving. This rising tide of prosperity gave a second life to the Roman Empire in the East. At just the moment when the empire of Old Rome in the West had begun to teeter, the provincials of the Roman East had created what Sir Fergus Millar has pertinently described as a "*Greek* Roman Empire."[7]

From the Mediterranean to a Third World: Syria and Egypt

As the sequence of these chapters shows, my work on the "holy poor" led me first to the Christian communities established around the Mediterranean—in the Aegean, in Rome, around Antioch, and in Carthage. The establishment of a professional clergy and of a tradition of Christian teachers (supported by the laity as if they were members of the "holy poor") took place largely in the cities of the Mediterranean in the second and third centuries. This development coincided with the imperial crisis of the third century and with the related persecutions of the Christian church.

But already by the end of the third century (by the beginning of my third chapter) I found myself in a wider world. The late third, fourth, and fifth centuries AD witnessed the rise of the ascetic movement in non-Mediterranean regions, in Syria and in Egypt. (By "Syria" I do not mean only the territories of the modern state of Syria, but something far more extensive: a major cultural region of the Middle East, which stretched from the hills of eastern Turkey and of northern Iraq as far south as Jordan, Israel, and Palestine.) These two regions provided a dramatic new backdrop to an ancient issue. It is with these two regions that the remaining four chapters and conclusion of this book will be concerned. For it was among the holy men of Syria (in the wide sense) and the monks of Egypt that the issues of work and the holy poor first raised in the letters of Saint Paul were played out in their final and most dramatic form. Put very briefly: should monks work?

In some ways, I was struck by the continuity with the early Christian past of the issues that were so hotly debated in the earliest phases of the ascetic movement. Reading the literature of the monastic movement in Egypt, in Syria—and of other radical Christian groups—I found myself almost in a time warp. I was back once again in the days of Saint Paul. Each side cited Paul in support of its own position—whether to work or not to work. I soon realized that these citations of Paul were no mere "proof texts," taken at random from the letters of the Apostle. They condensed points of tension that reached back directly to the earliest days of the Christian church. These tensions were still unresolved in the days of the first monks. Paul was vividly present to the monks of the fourth century, not as some distant authority figure, but because the issues that he had addressed were still present to the Christian communities of their own time.

Indeed, no barrier (such as we often imagine from standard periodizations of church history) had come down to cut off the Christian churches of the fourth and fifth century East from the

Constantinople

A N A T O L I A

CAPPADOCIA

SEE INSET BELOW

Antioch • • Aleppo

Salamis

Orontes

Mediterranean Sea

Beirut •

Damascus •

HAURAN

PALESTINE

Gaza • • Jerusalem

Alexandria •

NEGEV

SCETIS
(WADI NATRUN)

Karanis •
Fayyum •

Nile

Hermopolis • • Antinoë

UPPER EGYPT

Atripe
(Sohag) •

Kellis •

• Deir el-Madina

DAKHLAH
OASIS

Esna •

ETHIOPIA

Red Sea

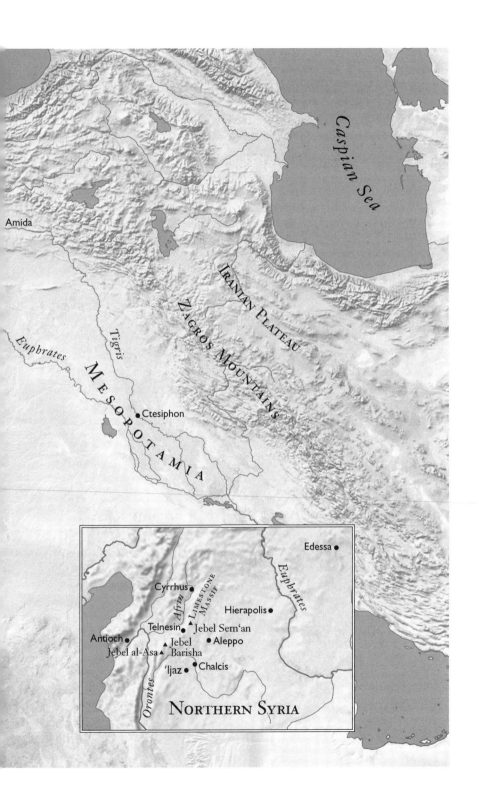

Caspian Sea

Amida

IRANIAN PLATEAU

ZAGROS MOUNTAINS

Euphrates

Tigris

MESOPOTAMIA

Ctesiphon

Edessa

Euphrates

Cyrrhus

LIMESTONE MASSIF

Afrin

Telnesin ▲

▲ Jebel Sem'an

Hierapolis

Antioch

Jebel al-Asa ▲

▲ Jebel Barisha

● Aleppo

'Ijaz ●

● Chalcis

Orontes

NORTHERN SYRIA

problems they had faced in the days of Saint Paul and of the early church. Throughout the first, second, and third centuries, Paul and his many vivid successors ensured that the issue of labor and the holy poor was prominent. But in the fourth and fifth centuries, what had always been a hot issue became, once again, incandescent. For the stakes were higher. Throughout Egypt and the Middle East, the monastic movement hung in the balance for a moment, undecided as to whether monks and nuns—as new, outstanding members of the holy poor—should work for their living or whether, like the Buddhist monks of northern India, of Central Asia, and of western China, they should live entirely from alms of the pious.

Furthermore, these debates took place against a background as vast as the issues that they now raised. They emerged in Christian regions that extended far beyond the Greco-Roman world, on which conventional accounts of the rise and expansion of Christianity usually concentrate. But by the year AD 300, the brightly lit world of the Mediterranean was flanked by another Christianity, associated primarily with Egypt and with the wide spaces of Syria. We are dealing with a great third world of ancient Christianity that stretched far to the east of Antioch, as far as the Caucasus and the Iranian plateau, and far to the south of Alexandria, as far as the Indian Ocean and the mountains of Ethiopia.

In this respect, I should make clear that, when I speak of "third world," readers should not think of the term "third world" as standing only, as it tends to do nowadays, for the impoverished regions of the globe. Rather, the phrase "third world" should carry with it the high hopes of the days when it was first used (as in the Bandung Conference of 1955) to conjure up the cultural as well as the political and economic resources of the recently freed, nonaligned nations, who were thought, at the time, to offer a fruitful alternative to the dire confrontation between the West and the Communist bloc. Flanking the Greco-Roman world (and all too often overlooked by those who studied Greek and Latin Christianity), the Christianities of Syria, Egypt, and the Caucasus were far from being the poor relatives of the West.

They stood, indeed, for a third option—for a reservoir of Christian thought and devotion whose depths we have only begun to plumb.

One of the great advances in the study of late antiquity has been the increased awareness of the role played by this third world in forming the religious culture of what had hitherto been called (somewhat unthinkingly) "the Greek East." The spectacular development, in recent decades, of the study of Syriac Christian literature has added nothing less than a new dimension to our conventional image of ancient Christianity.[8] This was a Christianity that had developed to one side of the Mediterranean, along routes that linked the Roman world to Mesopotamia, to Persia, and even to India. A series of gifted studies have also begun to do justice to the complexity of the relations between this distinctive regional culture and the Hellenistic civilization that had always coexisted alongside it and that came to be inextricably intertwined with it in the late antique period.[9] Similar, highly original, and differentiated work has been done for the mixed Greco-Coptic world of Egypt.[10]

These two traditions of recent scholarship have made late antique Syria and Egypt available to us as never before. But, of course, it is always easier to acclaim breakthroughs in scholarship than it is to follow them up by incorporating them in one's own work. For these breakthroughs are the result of highly specialized learning and of hard-won expertise that few of us possess. Yet, I trust that expert readers will forgive me if I try to take advantage of the horizons opened up by recent scholarship in Coptic and Syriac to look again at the ascetic movements of that long-neglected third world of Christianity.

I have been led to do this by a sense that Syria and Egypt have too often been studied in isolation from each other. I would suggest that we might gain something by looking at the extent to which they were inter-visible. The two regions are not often brought together in this way. Yet, if we look closely at the monastic experiments and at the monastic self-presentations of the one region we see that they are linked by a continuous muffled dialogue with those of the other. What often appears to be most distinctively, unthinkingly local (such as the Egyptian emphasis on the manual labor of monks) was, in reality, a considered response to alternatives that remained visible and attractive in other parts of the Christian East.

The need to stress inter-visibility not only involves overcoming the crudely drawn geographical boundaries that have tended to cut Syria off from Egypt. We also have to look at the inter-visibility between differing strands in the Christian ascetic movement itself. We have tended to divide and to compartment these differing strands according to theological principles. We assume that some groups—such as the missionaries of the Manichaean movement (whom we will meet in chap. 3)—were totally beyond the pale of Christian orthodoxy, and so played little or no role in the evolution of Christian ascetic practice. We also tend to assume that the holy men of Syria were, somehow, wilder, woolier (and more prone to theological error) than were the stolid monks of Egypt—and, hence, that the monastic experiments of Syria were, somehow, more "archaic" and for that reason less destined to last than were the solid hermitages and monasteries of Egypt.

What we need to do, rather, is to line up these different variants of ascetic Christianity as equals in confronting a common early Christian dilemma—how much, if at all, were a special category of Christians entitled to the support of others? Seen according to this fundamental choice, shared, in differing ways, by Christians of all persuasions, the various ascetic movements of the Christian East fall into place. They can be seen as different but clearly inter-visible attempts to handle a dilemma that was as old as Saint Paul—indeed, as old as civilization itself: who gets to work, who can claim to be free, and on what terms? And, hence, our book ends with the contrast between the work-free holy men of Syria and the working monks of Egypt. As in a much older world (in the days of Ramses II and the Eighteenth Dynasty of ancient Egypt), the Nile and the Fertile Crescent reached out, once again, to touch each other, and to define themselves one against the other.

If this account of the different course taken by the Christian ascetic movements in Syria and Egypt on the crucial issue of labor brings to the reader a greater sense of the spiritual wealth of those two great Christian regions, and of the decisive role that they played, in this period, in determining the future of Christianity in East and West, I will be contented. If this book reminds us, also, of the extent to which these distinctive forms of Christianity have added a unique flavor to the Christianity of our own, Western world, it will go a little way to repay the all-too-easily forgotten debt that we owe to them. But further still, if this book also reminds us of how the deep roots and rich traditions of these differing Oriental Christianities (now, once again, in great peril in so many regions of the Middle East) have contributed both to our own civilization and to the diversity of the lands in which they first blossomed and still hope to survive, then I will feel that, as a historian, I will have done my duty.

Peter Brown, August 18, 2014

Treasure in Heaven

1

"Treasure in Heaven" and "The Poor among the Saints": Jesus and Paul—Leadership and the Escape from Labor

Jesus and Paul

In this chapter, I will begin by going back to what the Christians whom we are studying in this book considered to be the basics. I will draw attention to two traditions of religious giving that came to lie side by side in the New Testament.

First, we have the abrupt words of Jesus to the Rich Young Man: *"go and sell all that thou hast and give to the poor, and then thou shalt have treasure in heaven"* (Matt. 19:21). This challenge was associated with the journeys of Jesus of Nazareth and his disciples in Galilee and Judaea (in modern Israel and Palestine) around AD 30. It would echo through the centuries, among Christians, as if above place and time. As a result, it takes a considerable effort of the imagination to unravel its implications to Christians of the first centuries of the church.

But we also meet a very different tradition of giving connected with the activities of Saint Paul in the cities of the Aegean (on the coasts of modern Greece and Turkey). The letters ascribed to Saint Paul (which, we must remember, all early Christians accepted as a single block, all written by Saint Paul) reveal him at work in one of the best-documented exercises in fund-raising in the ancient world. Furthermore, Paul's activities in organizing a collection to support *the poor among the saints in Jerusalem* (Rom. 15:26) went hand in hand with a debate as to the extent to which "apostles" (such as Paul)—and, by extension, other Christian religious leaders—were entitled to support from the communities to whom they ministered.

Within a little over a century, in around AD 150, these two

faces of early Christianity—the sayings of Jesus and the letters of Paul—had come together in the same canon of the Christian scriptures, in the New Testament. On the one hand, we have a timeless call to renunciation, linked to the promise of *treasure in heaven*. On the other hand, we have a feverish correspondence concerning the movement of money in the Christian communities. In Paul's letters, wealth was not there to be renounced. It was there to be used. Furthermore, it was to be used as much to support religious leaders as to support *the poor among the saints* on whose behalf Paul's appeal had first been launched.

The two traditions are very different from each other. But it was between these two traditions that Christian thought on religious giving swung, like a great pendulum, from the days of Jesus and the first missionary journeys of Saint Paul to the age of Constantine and far beyond. A complete study of the use of wealth in the Christian churches has to take account of both traditions. So let us now deal—inevitably briefly—with each of them in turn.

"Treasures for Below . . . Treasures for Above"

First: let us go back to the sayings of Jesus. The most dramatic of these sayings was addressed to a rich young man: *"Jesus said unto him: If thou wilt be perfect, go and sell all that thou hast and give to the poor, and then thou shalt have treasure in heaven: and come and follow me"* (Matt. 19:21; cf. Mark 10:21 and Luke 18:22). Jesus was also believed to have said much the same to his disciples: *"Sell your possessions and give alms; provide yourselves with purses that do not grow old, with a treasure in the heavens that does not fail, where no thief approaches and no moth destroys"* (Luke 12:33).

The dramatic effect of these sayings on well-to-do Christians throughout the ages has been studied exhaustively.[1] But, in order to understand the full implications of the sayings of Jesus for the attitudes of early Christians toward wealth and the poor, we need to look more carefully at them.

What struck contemporaries in these sayings was the counterfactual assertion that *treasure in heaven* would be gained through the loss of *treasure on earth*. This idea was not unique to Christi-

anity. Similar notions circulated in Jewish circles. In the Jerusalem Talmud (which was probably put together in the late fourth
century AD), Monobazos, the Jewish king of Adiabene on the Euphrates in the early first century AD, was said to have spent his
fortune on providing food for the poor in Jerusalem. His infuri-
ated relatives accused him of living down to his name, which was
derived from the word *bazaz*—to plunder. They accused Monobazos of plundering the earthly inheritance of his family. He answered them at length: "My fathers laid up treasures for below,
but I have laid up treasures for above. . . . They laid up treasures
in a place over which the hand of man may prevail: I in a place
over which no hand can prevail. . . . My fathers laid up treasures
useful in this world, I for the world to come."[2]

Monobazos's speech was accepted by the rabbis as an appropriate justification of his pious giving. Yet, in contrast to Jews and
Christians, pagans of the second and third centuries reacted to the
idea of "treasure in heaven" with studied incredulity. At the end
of the third century AD, the great pagan philosopher Porphyry
(who was born in Caesarea Maritima in Palestine and had studied
with the great Neoplatonist Plotinus in Rome) wrote, in his treatise *Against the Christians*, that this saying could not have come
from Jesus. Rather, Porphyry opined, the saying must have been
invented by poor people, with the intention of persuading the
rich to give all their money to them, *ek toiautés kenophônias*—"as
a result of such airhead talk." Porphyry added that this airhead
talk had begun to affect the rich of his own times. He wrote that
he had heard only recently of some well-to-do Christian ladies
who had impoverished themselves, and made themselves a burden to others, by taking this passage literally.[3]

A century later, in AD 362, Christian ideas about placing treasure in heaven through the renunciation of wealth were the object of a jibe by the pagan emperor Julian the Apostate. Angered
by the Christians of Edessa (a frontier city with a major, well-
endowed church), Julian decided to confiscate the funds of the
church. With the somewhat elephantine humor to which he was
prone, Julian claimed that he was doing the Christians a favor
by stripping the church of its possessions! "Since by their most

admirable law they are bidden to sell all and give to the poor so that they may attain more easily to the kingdom of the skies, in order to help those persons in that effort, I have ordered that all their funds, namely, that belong to the church of the people of Edessa, are to be taken over."[4]

To Join Heaven and Earth

Late antique pagans might be suspicious of the notion of "treasure in heaven." But we are simply embarrassed. When one turns to the current scholarship on this theme, we find that the idea of "treasure in heaven" has come to be surrounded by a loud silence. Neither in the Catholic *Dictionnaire de la Spiritualité* nor in the Protestant *Theologische Realenzyklopädie* is there an entry on "trésor" or on "Schatz." Nor can such an article be found in the *Oxford Dictionary of the Christian Church* or in the recent *Oxford Dictionary of the Jewish Religion*.

The few studies addressed to the Jewish and Christian notion of "treasure in heaven" approach it with ill-disguised discomfort. One such study, by Klaus Koch, insists that Jesus must have meant something very different from the meanings that came to be attached to his words in later centuries. Belief in the direct accumulation of treasure in heaven through almsgiving on earth was dismissed out of hand by Koch: it was "für den Protestanten eine abscheuliche Vorstellung"—a notion abhorrent to any Protestant.[5]

Modern Jewish scholars are no less embarrassed. Faced by the tale of King Monobazos, the great Talmudic scholar Ephraim Urbach confessed that it was difficult for him to see "traces of a more refined doctrine . . . [or, indeed, any] sublimation of the materialistic simile of collecting treasures above through squandering them below" in King Monobazos's "prolonged and monotonous explanation."[6]

Nowadays, indeed, the thought of transferring mere money from earth to heaven strikes us as something more than a harmless exercise of the imagination. Rather, it has the quality of an off-color joke. It joins two zones of the imagination—that of money and that of religion—which modern persons tend to keep apart.

But if we are to understand the imaginative energy that drove religious giving in Christian circles in this period and in the Middle Ages, we have to recapture something of the weight and the distinctive profile of the notion of a transfer of wealth from earth to heaven implied in the words of Jesus and of King Monobazos. Let us try to do this for a moment.

To begin with, we must defamiliarize the sayings of Jesus. As modern persons, we tend to think that we know what he meant. We assume that the notion of placing treasure in heaven was no more than a stirring metaphor. It was chosen by Jesus so as to encourage heroic indifference to wealth and the redistribution of wealth by the rich for the betterment of the poor.

But these are modern reactions. In early Christianity, a considerably wider conglomerate of notions gathered around the words of Jesus. Among these notions, the redistribution of wealth through giving to the poor was undeniably present. The great Christian theologian Origen of Alexandria (ca. 185–254) claimed to have read an alternative version of the challenge of Jesus to the Rich Young Man in an apocryphal Gospel of the Hebrews. In this version, there was no mention of "treasure in heaven." Nor was the Rich Young Man told to "sell all." Jesus merely told him to treat his fellow believers more generously.[7] The message of the Gospel of the Hebrews was as banal as any modern version of the encounter between Jesus and the Rich Young Man. But what struck most early Christian readers and hearers was something rather different. In this one saying, Jesus had brought together two starkly opposed incommensurables and had declared that the one might be transformed into the other through a form of exchange that flouted all the rules of social common sense: heaven and earth, rich and poor (each group thought to be immeasurably distant one from the other) were brought together through a heroic act of giving to the poor.[8]

Not only did wealth—with all its sinister overtones of gross and weighty matter, touched by transience and death—join the unbearable lightness of a world beyond the stars. The primal joining of heaven and earth was mirrored in society itself. The starkly antithetical poles of rich and poor were brought together, through almsgiving. Through these two primal joinings, the greatest gulf of all—that between God and humankind—was healed. In the well-chosen words of Gary Anderson: "Charity was . . . an act that established a contact point between the believer and God."[9]

The Elm and the Vine: The Joining of Rich and Poor in Early Christianity

What was it that made the notion of the joining of incommensurables so attractive to the early Christian communities? Let me suggest that these communities found, in the idea of the joining of heaven and earth and rich and poor, an expression of solidarity across real (or imagined) social cleavages.

These social cleavages were not necessarily very wide in real life. In this respect, we must be more than usually careful when reading early Christian writings on the relations between rich and poor within the Christian communities. They do not give us a realistic description of the social structure of these communities. For they wrote under the influence of a powerful conceptual polarity. Like heaven and earth, rich and poor were presented as separate. What mattered was that the one was not the other. But this did not in any way mean that, in the Christian communities, the rich were divided by an immense social gulf from the poor.

If anything, this was not the case in the Christian communities of the first and second centuries. What little we know about them suggests that they harbored a wider range of persons than we had once thought. They did not contain very many rich members. But nor were they drawn only from the very poor. Where scholars differ is in estimating the width of the social spectrum to which Christians belonged at this time. Was it wide, touching persons of different classes and of very different levels of culture, or was it narrow, confined largely to the poor?

Some scholars (such as Gerd Theissen and Wayne Meeks) have presented the first Christians as relatively well-to-do, almost as "middle class."[10] Other scholars have reacted sharply against what they regard as an overcomfortable view. Justin Megitt and Steven Friesen have argued forcefully that the first Christian communities were far from being "middle class." For Megitt and Friesen, the early Christians lay on the wrong side of the precipice that separated the rich from the vast majority of the poor in the Roman Empire. Megitt and Friesen imagine the Roman Empire to have been a relentlessly polarized society. In their view, there was little social differentiation beneath the level of the rich. Not to be rich was to be very, very poor. In their opinion, the letters of Paul revealed the churches to be organizations of the poor. They struggled to stay afloat through ingenious schemes of mutual support. There was nothing comfortable or "middle class" about them.[11]

This scholarly debate has remained unresolved. This is largely because the Christian writings of the time cast little light upon the real social structure of the Christian communities. Their aim was not to describe the actual relations between rich and poor in the churches. It was to present their social world as if it were structured around a dramatic polarity of "rich" and "poor," which only the magic of Christian almsgiving could bring together.

But it was precisely this emphasis on the joining of opposites which proved most acceptable to the Christian communities of the late first and second centuries. Like their Jewish neighbors, the early Christians were a group that was socially differentiated but by no means brutally polarized. What they needed were images of solidarity that stressed the joining of distinct and potentially opposed groups: the greater the imagined distance between rich and poor, the more triumphant was the overcoming of this distance in a united Christian community.

Not all these images of solidarity were drawn from the sayings of Jesus. A further, arresting image was used in the book of parables, written by Hermas, a prophet in the Christian community of Rome, in around AD 140.[12] Walking in the Roman Campagna, Hermas was struck by the sight of a vine trained over an elm tree: "I am thinking about the elm and the vine, that they are excellently suited to each other. . . . This vine bears fruit, but the elm is an unfruitful stock. Yet this vine, except it climbs up the elm, cannot bear fruit. The rich man has much wealth, but in the things of the Lord he is poor, being distracted by his riches. But the poor man, being supplied by the rich, makes intercession for him."[13]

It is interesting to note that the rabbis faced a similar juxtaposition of potentially irreconcilable groups within the Jewish community. For the rabbis, these groups were not simply the rich and the poor. They were also the scholars and the ignorant common people, the *ammei ha-aretz*—effectively, the learned men of leisure (the rabbis) and their hardworking fellow Jews. Each group needed to be reminded that they depended on each other through an organic, almost subliminal bond: "This people [of Israel] is like unto a vine; its branches are the wealthy, its clusters are the scholars, its leaves are the common people. . . . Let the clusters pray for the leaves, for were it not for the leaves, the clusters could not exist."[14]

In both cases, the image of the vine spoke to the wish for solidarity between the different groups within a religious community. But the image did more than this. It implied that the community was held together by a spiritual exchange—by an exchange of prayer for wealth. This exchange did not necessarily benefit only the poor. In the parables of Hermas, it was the poor who repaid the rich with their prayers. In the Talmud, by contrast, it was the scholars who prayed for the mass of unlearned Jews.

In either case, we can see the emergence of the notion of a spiritual exchange—an exchange of material for spiritual goods. This exchange pushed to the fore any group of persons (Christian poor or Jewish scholars) who were believed to offer the invisible gifts of prayer and wisdom in exchange for the visible gift of material support. But whose prayers would be considered to be most effective? And what role would they play within the Christian churches? In order to understand this, we should go back to the days of Saint Paul.

"They Would Have Us Remember the Poor": The Pauline Collection

Paul's letters are the earliest documents of Christianity. In the opinion of most scholars, they were written between AD 49 and 55. Unlike Jesus, Paul did not speak of the renunciation of wealth. Rather, his letters were notably concerned with money. In the words of Dieter Georgi, in his challenging book *Remembering the Poor: The History of the Pauline Collection for Jerusalem,* "The authentic writings of Paul contain some of the most elaborate literary reflections on the flow of money surviving from the ancient world."[15]

In these letters we find Paul at work organizing a series of collections (Gal. 2:1–10, 1 Cor. 16:1–4, 2 Cor. 8–9, and Rom. 15:14–32). These collections were made for a group known as *"the poor among the saints in Jerusalem"* (Rom. 15:26). The collections had been instituted (according to Paul) in response to the demand of the Christian community in Jerusalem *"that they would have us remember the poor"* (Gal. 2:10). Furthermore, in other parts of the letters ascribed to him, Paul defended at great length his own behavior in alternately seeking and refusing financial support while teaching and traveling (1 Cor. 9:3–18, 2 Cor. 11:7–12, and 2 Thess. 3:7–10).

Altogether, Paul's letters give us an unexpected glimpse of a great fund-raiser in action. They also provided later readers with a clear-cut statement of the notion of a spiritual exchange such as would exercise Christians in all succeeding centuries. Speaking to the Corinthians of his entitlement to support as a teacher, Paul wrote: *"If we have sown spiritual good among you, is it too much if we reap your material benefits?"* (1 Cor. 9:11).

These aspects of the life and writings of Paul have been exhaustively studied of late.[16] So let me step back a little from the details of Paul's collections for the saints, and from his own complex attitude to receiving financial support from those to whom he ministered, to consider some of the wider factors that gave resonance among Christians to his writings both at the time and in future centuries.

For, in the case of Paul, we can see the emergence of a dilemma. A collection made for *"the poor among the saints"* quickly escalated into a discussion of what demands could be made on ordinary believers, who worked for their living, in order to support the activities of Paul and his helpers as organizers of collections for the poor, as missionaries, and as teachers. Discussion of alms for the many quickly became a discussion also of financial support for the few.

Here we must always bear in mind that the financial support of religious leaders had always been a charged issue for ancient persons. Saint Paul lived under the shadow of a well-known negative stereotype. He knew very well that he could be seen, by his critics and by outsiders, as a charismatic fund-raiser for whom religion was a way of making money. Later pagan readers of the letters of Paul had no doubt about this. They concluded that he had been the usual sort of religious entrepreneur. In the opinion of the philosopher Porphyry, the letters of Paul were written "in a spirit of vain glory, with financial gain in mind."[17]

Paul and those around him knew that such suspicions had to be answered. A vivid tableau, carefully presented in the Acts of the Apostles, condensed the issues that had been brought to a head by Paul's activities. In AD 55, Paul landed at Samos on his way to deliver the funds that he had collected for the church in Jerusalem. He was met at Miletus by the elders of the church of Ephesus. These elders were potentially hostile. They were on the alert for charismatic spongers. The first thing that Paul did when faced by such a group was to show them his hands. These were the hard hands of a man who, despite his religious calling, had continued to work for a living: *"I coveted no man's silver or gold or apparel . . . these hands ministered to my necessities, and to those who were with me. In all things I have shown you that by so toiling one must help the weak, remembering the words of the Lord Jesus, how He said: 'It is more blessed to give than to receive'"* (Acts 20:33–35).

This rare appeal, on Paul's part, to the direct words of Jesus (to a saying of Jesus's that does not appear in any Gospel) shows how important it was to steer clear of the accusation that he had lived off the toil of his followers. The fact that the incident itself and Paul's speech may have been put together in retrospect (or may even have been a fiction that projected later concerns back onto the lifetime of the Apostle) only adds weight to its message. It was a highly charged scene. In all future centuries, Christians looked back to it as the exemplary self-portrait of a man who had not taken the easy way out. Paul had gone out of his way to combine his missionary activities with hard work, shown by his hard hands.

Altogether, Christians faced two problems: how to *remember the poor* through religious giving, and how to pay for their own religious leaders. Already in the time of Paul, we can see the emergence of an ambiguity that would continue from this time until the Reformation (and, indeed, up to today). Who are the poor? Are they the "economic" poor or are they, rather, the "holy" poor—*the poor among the saints*? And who are the "holy poor"? Do the "holy" poor include the religious leaders (bishops and clergymen) who, as part of their duties, looked after the "economic" poor? Last but not least: do the "poor" who required support also include more vivid figures than the clergy—chosen souls, monks and nuns, on whose prayers and wisdom Christians all over the Mediterranean and the Middle East would come to depend in the course of the fourth and fifth centuries? This dilemma runs, like a tensed spring, from one end of this book to the other, joining the four centuries that stretched between the days of Saint Paul and the rise of monasticism in Syria and Egypt.

Christian communities had to decide whether those who gave up their time as teachers, as missionaries, and (later) as church officials (thereby sacrificing their earning power or their ability to look after their own properties) were entitled to support as if they were members of the "poor"—indeed, as if they were members of the "poor" par excellence. In the words of Denise Kimber Buell, already by the end of the first century AD, the tendency was well under way to treat many persons other than the poor—apostles, prophets, teachers, organizers, and distributors of funds—as each of them "some kind of special insider," each in need of special material support.[18]

It was not always easy to provide this support. We can see the problems that faced a Christian community in a vivid text from the region of Antioch—the *Didache: The Teaching of the Apostles*. The *Didache* was written at some time in the late first or early second century. In it, the poor posed no problems. What concerned the members of the community were the claims of the "holy poor." Wandering "prophets" made claims on the hospitality and on the pockets of believers in return for their inspired teaching. These figures were subjected to firm scrutiny. Believers were told not to be too hasty in making contributions to collections made on behalf of such persons: "Let your alms sweat into your hands, until you shall have learned to whom to give."[19]

Prophets who were accepted as genuine were welcome— but only for two days: "but if he stays three days, he is a false prophet. . . . From his ways therefore the false prophet shall be recognized. And no prophet who orders up a table [a collective feast] under the inspiration of the Holy Spirit shall eat it for himself. If he does this, he is a false prophet."[20]

It is hardly surprising that so many early Christian texts, from the letters of Paul onward, "reflect the strenuous ideological work of justifying the support of such anomalous figures."[21]

"Hard-Handed Men": Religion and Labor

We must remember that this dilemma was not unique to the early church. Rather, early Christians found themselves swept into a silent revolution which, already in the first and second centuries AD, marked the beginning of the end of the ancient world. Put very briefly, the quickening of the tempo of religious life throughout the Mediterranean was accompanied by an unprecedented "democratization" of religious expertise and of religious leadership. This development, in turn, was related to the overall prosperity of the Roman Empire. A general rise in economic activity and in the availability of surplus money enabled relatively humble persons to create small religious associations, and to embark on careers as ritual experts, mystagogues, preachers, and founders of new cults.[22]

TREASURE IN HEAVEN

In many sections of the Roman world, religion became a *carrière ouverte aux talents* to an extent that had not been the case previously. Persons of the lower and middling classes, who found it difficult to support themselves in normal conditions, entered with gusto into the high enterprise of religion. Not being persons of independent means, they had to be supported by others. Hence a crisis that affected Judaism and many pagan cults quite as much as it affected the Christian churches.

In measuring the extent of this revolution, we should never forget how comfortably *de haut en bas* the traditional religious establishments of the ancient world had been. Religious speculation had usually been regarded as the preserve of philosophers and of scribes who came from the wealthy classes. Their wealth was assumed to have given them the leisure to engage in the elevating and time-consuming business of religion. For they were not held, as were the majority of their fellows, in the permafrost of *ponos*—of drudgery.[23]

In the social common sense of all ancient persons, *ponos*, drudgery—and not poverty—was the true antithesis to "wealth." In the words of an acute summary of the social values of the ancient Greeks: "The criterion was not a given standard of wealth but the need to work. A Greek was wealthy if he could live without having to work, poor if he did not have enough to live on without working."[24]

As always with the self-representations of traditional societies, this crisp summary (and the sources on which it is based) should not be taken at face value. The sources never offered a comprehensive description of classical society in all its complexity. But the message of the social representations that we encounter in classical texts was clear. The identification of "true" wealth with freedom from labor acted as a "keep off the grass" notice. It told the nonrich, in no uncertain terms, from what activities they were debarred.

One did not have to be economically "poor" to be subject to *ponos*. It was quite possible to be prosperous but still to be obliged by circumstances to take pains to preserve one's wealth. But whether they were relatively rich or truly poor, those who had not reached the point of "liftoff" from financial cares that enabled them to abandon work were expected to resign themselves to the fact that they could not join the company of the thoughtful. They could not become intellectual or religious leaders. The taint of labor lay upon them.

On this matter, the Hellenized Jewish author of the *Wisdom of Ben Sira/Ecclesiasticus* spoke for the elites of the Greco-Roman world as a whole: "The wisdom of a learned man cometh by opportunity of leisure: and he that hath little business shall become wise. How can he get wisdom that holdeth the plough . . . that driveth oxen, and is occupied in their labours?" (Ecclus. 38:24–25).[25]

The image of the average person as disqualified from intellectual activity by the fact of labor was a particularly tenacious social stereotype. It was shared by all members of the classically educated upper classes. It passed into Christian circles. Writing at the end of the fourth century AD, Gregory of Nyssa (ca. 335–95), the mystically inclined brother of the great Basil of Caesarea (ca. 330–79), began his attack on the Arian writer Eunomius by pointing out that Eunomius's father had been a farmer. He had spent his life "bent over the plow, expending much pain [much *ponos*] over a little plot of land."[26]

The farmer's son, Eunomius, was self-educated. Gregory claimed that such a person had no right to claim membership of the exclusive club of those devoted to high thought. Of course, what was galling to Gregory was that the reality was very different. Despite his relatively humble origins, Eunomius had spent a comfortable and well-connected life in Antioch and Constantinople on the strength of his talents as a religious expert. He showed that the pursuit of religion paid off, in the face of the old-world snobbery of his opponents.[27] The success of Eunomius was a sign of the times.

The world of upper-class leisure, such as that praised by ben Sira—and still implied by Gregory of Nyssa—seemed to be an unchallenged aspect of the ancient world. But it was very much not what we meet in the first centuries of Christianity. We catch a glimpse of the average representatives of Palestinian Christian-

TREASURE IN HEAVEN

ity in a strange encounter that took place in around AD 90. Traveling through Palestine in the wake of the Jewish Revolt, the emperor Domitian was told that the relatives of Jesus of Nazareth were still living. Concerned that the family of a self-proclaimed Messiah and potential king of the Jews might still be dangerous, he summoned them to his tent. They turned out to be small farmers. They were by no means members of the landless poor. They were capable of supporting themselves and even a few servants on holdings of around twenty-five acres.[28] They were men of *ponos*, and they could prove it. They did exactly what Saint Paul was said to have done a generation earlier: "They showed him their hands, bringing forward as proof of their toil the hardness of their bodies and the calluses inflicted on their hands by incessant labor. . . . Domitian . . . despising them as beneath his notice, let them free."[29]

The emperor was reassured by what he saw. Such persons, caught in drudgery, could do him no harm. Fifteen hundred years later, William Shakespeare, in his *Midsummer Night's Dream*, still reflected the mood of persons such as ben Sira and Domitian. The humble craftsmen of Athens, assembled by Duke Theseus to produce a play, are presented as harmless and vaguely ludicrous persons. They are "Hard-handed men . . . / Which never labored in their minds till now."[30]

But, in fact, the emperor Domitian had glimpsed the future. In the succeeding centuries, "hard-handed men" found themselves set loose, in increasing numbers, to "labor in their minds." In a brilliant recent survey of the religious world of the second and third centuries, Richard Gordon has reminded us of "the attraction in a highly stratified, highly unequal society of specifically religious roles as a means of acquiring social capital and thus social recognition."[31]

The development of the Christian churches in this period confirms Gordon's observation. It was a development in which the ability to raise and allocate money played a decisive role, so as to support those who had taken on religious roles. In these decisive centuries (the second and third centuries), the Christian clergy and, if in a different manner, the Jewish rabbinate developed systems of religious giving by the faithful that supported an increasing number of persons whose lives would otherwise have been given over to the drudgery of labor. It is to the working out of this potentially problematic dynamic in the Christian churches of the second and third centuries AD that we must now turn.

2

"Do It through the Bishop": Tricksters, Bishops, and Teachers, AD 200–300

From Jesus to Peregrinus: The Image of the Religious Entrepreneur in the Second Century AD

In our last chapter we began with the sayings of Jesus that promised *treasure in heaven* to those who renounced their possessions. We examined the manner in which this phrase implied the possibility of a mysterious joining of incommensurables. Not only would heaven and earth be joined through dramatic acts of renunciation or of generosity. But also on earth itself, within the Christian community, the equally distant poles of rich and poor would be joined through almsgiving.

Then we followed the theme of the joining of opposites in the parables of the prophet Hermas, who addressed the Christian community in Rome around AD 140. What Hermas proposed, in his vivid image of the fruitful vine supported by the infertile elm tree, was the notion of the organic symbiosis of rich and poor within the Christian community. The rich supported the poor in return for their prayers, much as ordinary Jews were expected to support the Torah study of the rabbis.

In other words, we are looking at the emergence of a binary model of the religious community. This binary model implied what is best called a "spiritual exchange." One section of the Christian community supported the other with visible wealth in exchange for the invisible but potent spiritual benefit of prayer and other "spiritual" activities on their behalf.

This binary model had already been adumbrated in the letters of Saint Paul. Not only did Paul organize collections for a special kind of poor—for *the poor among the saints* in distant Jerusalem.

His activities raised the issue as to whether he also—or if not himself, then others—were entitled to financial support from the communities to whom he ministered. Writing to the Christian community in Corinth, Paul justified this arrangement with a vivid image: *"If we have sown spiritual good among you, is it too much if we reap material benefits from you?"* (1 Cor. 9:11). Altogether, the stream of giving that flowed toward the poor alone, according to the primordial sayings of Jesus, had become divided. Some of this stream now flowed toward the leaders of the Christian movement and similar privileged persons.

Furthermore, as we saw, the notion of material support for religious leaders had repercussions in Roman society as a whole. For such support enabled persons who, in normal life, would have been tied to the drudgery of labor to shrug off the restraints of work. They could embark on exciting careers as religious experts. Supported by their followers, they threatened to "gate-crash" the preserves of the rich, by offering religious guidance and inspiration that had once been considered the monopoly of the leisured classes.

To members of the leisured classes, this was a far from welcome development. In the second century AD, a withering scorn for those who made money out of religious enterprises was a characteristic reflex of those lucky few who did not need to make money in the first place. It was taken for granted in such circles that many persons embarked on religious activities so as to escape work. To set oneself up as a sorcerer, as a diviner, or as the founder of a new cult was simply one disreputable expedient among many others by which members of the laborious classes tried to buck the system.

To take one notable instance. In the mid-second century, the pagan philosopher Celsus presented Jesus in just these terms. The son of an unwed mother, Jesus had been forced to live on his wits: "Because he was poor, he hired himself out as a workman in Egypt, and there tried his hand at certain magical powers . . . he returned full of conceit because of these powers, and on account of them gave himself the title of God." Celsus had seen it all before. Jesus was just one of those "who go about begging and say they are sons of God who have come from above." His disciples were no better. They were "infamous men . . . who had not had even a primary education." They moved "hither and thither, collecting a means of livelihood in a disgraceful and importunate way."[1] They were plainly in it for the money.

We have already seen how the negative stereotype of the religious leader as an avaricious fraud had overshadowed the career of Paul. He took great pains to avoid being branded as a trickster. Others were less scrupulous than Paul had been. Writing in around AD 170, Lucian, the Greek satirist, provided one of the first glimpses by an outsider into the inner workings of a Christian community. It was not a flattering glimpse.

If we are to believe Lucian, the eccentric Cynic philosopher Peregrinus had set himself up for a time among Christians. He became "prophet, cult-leader, head of the community. . . . He interpreted and explained some of their books and even composed many." As a result, so Lucian claimed, the wily Peregrinus lived in luxury, even when he was put in prison as a Christian: "For their first lawgiver [Jesus] persuaded them that they are all brothers one to another. . . . So if any charlatan and trickster comes among them, he quickly acquires sudden wealth by imposing upon simple folk."[2] Peregrinus did not last long among the Christians. A maverick to the last, he committed suicide in AD 165 by burning himself alive, close to the crowds gathered at the Olympic Games.

We would be unwise to take caricatures such as those of Celsus and Lucian as exact records of religious activity in the second-century Roman world. We need not imagine that the roads were filled overnight with upwardly mobile religious entrepreneurs. What we can say is that these stereotypes came to be mobilized with exceptional vigor in the course of the second century. They were used as exclusionary devices. They were intended to disqualify persons, many of whom were far from being out-and-out tricksters, money-grubbers, or social climbers.

This mobilization of stereotypes pointed to a tense situation. The intelligentsia itself had come to be divided. Christians were already present among the subelites—the writers and purveyors of knowledge who depended on the patronage of the great. What appear, at first sight, to be descriptions of Christians as total outsiders often reveal the exact opposite. Celsus, Lucian, and others were attempting to exclude and disqualify Christian intellectuals, many of whom already belonged to the same brittle and competitive class as they did.

By the middle of the second century, for a pagan to talk down the Christian communities as made up of simpleminded illiterates was not to describe them accurately. Rather, such stereotypes hinted at a religious and intellectual civil war among the subelites. Christians were part of these subelites. They vied with their pagan peers in presenting themselves as teachers, spiritual guides, and self-styled philosophers.[3]

In this way, the flamboyant sponger Peregrinus, quite as much as the acutely sensitive fund-raiser Paul, was a sign of the future. By offering support to persons who, previously, had been excluded from participation in the religious debates of their time through the necessity of work, money had begun to talk. And, in the second and third centuries, it talked increasingly about religion. So let us now see where this money came from. Let us look at the manner in which money was raised and allocated within the Christian communities of this time.

"Like a Beggar, Who Takes and Gives Nothing in Return": Reciprocity and Its Remedies in Christianity and Judaism

As the cases of Paul and Peregrinus show, the careers of religious leaders in the first and second centuries were closely monitored by contemporaries. Hostile accounts of their antics provide vivid reading for modern scholars. But these individual cases do not explain the extreme care that was taken to ensure that wealth circulated in the right manner and on a regular basis within the Christian churches. The continued efforts of the Christian churches to *remember the poor* took place in an atmosphere of constant questioning and regulation. Why was that so?

In the first place, the Christian poor were no longer only the distant *poor among the saints* of Jerusalem of whom Paul wrote.

Rich Christian communities continued to send money to other churches. But, by and large, the "poor" were the local poor of each Christian community. They were not necessarily strangers. Nor were they an anonymous mass of the destitute. In the second and third centuries, Christian charity remained intensely inward looking. It rarely extended to pagans. Rather, the "poor" tended to be fellow believers down on their luck. Hence the importance, in the Christian churches, of the care of the poor, of widows and orphans. For these persons were, as often as not, the spouses and offspring of former male members in good standing in the local church. The care of the poor, therefore, was almost a "family" matter. How it was conducted affected the structure and self-image of every Christian community.

As a result, Christian charity to the poor involved far more than the occasional gesture of compassion. The manner in which charity was given, and above all, the issues that were raised by its administration, had immediate repercussions on the self-awareness of each Christian group. For Christian charity posed a sociological conundrum of the first order: how to give generously within a religious community without subjecting the recipients of such gifts to the normal expectations of a quid pro quo that were current in ancient society.

One should not underestimate the seriousness of this concern. It is easy to forget how charged with meaning the act of giving was in all aspects of the social life of the Roman Empire. Wealth itself was blatant. It was not hidden in the anonymity of modern banking systems. Giving also tended to be blatant. It was the way in which the wealthy showed their power and, at the same time, bought support and protection from the envy of others. And there were always hands that reached out to take—whether these were the overpowering hands of emperors from on top or the ever-insistent hands of clients from below. In this cacophony of obligations and demands, any group that evolved a distinctive code of giving and receiving was sure to attract attention. The extent of Christian giving and the manner in which it was organized and discussed within the Christian community were sufficiently unusual to attract the attention of outsiders such as

Lucian and (according to Lucian) the greed of tricksters such as Peregrinus. Let us see why this was so.

Seen from the outside, Christian charity was a markedly "countercultural" activity. It deliberately flouted the expectations of a society that thought of itself as being held together by iron laws of reciprocity. To give to the poor on a regular basis was to throw money into a social void. The second-century dreambook of Artemidoros of Daldis made that clear. To dream that one had given money to a beggar was a very bad omen. It foretold death: "For Death is like a beggar, who takes and gives nothing in return."[4]

Yet this was precisely what Christians insisted on doing. To non-Christians this might seem a whimsical waste of good money on persons whose gratitude counted for nothing. But it was hailed by Christians as a moment of supreme freedom. Not only was such giving imagined to bring together heaven and earth, rich and poor. It broke a crucial link in the fetters of normal society, ruled as it was by seemingly relentless calculations of mutual obligation. To give without expecting a return was a magnificently gratuitous, liberating act.

As a result, Christian giving to the poor not only relieved the distress of fellow believers. It also helped to create a little utopia among them. It was a utopia such as non-Christian urban sophisticates had also liked to imagine. For example: Dio Chrysostomos (who wrote at the end of the first century) imagined that a society based on free giving had survived among the farmers of old-world Euboea. Their spontaneous generosity to passing strangers greatly impressed him. As Dio pointed out, these were not like the gifts of the rich, who always expected services of some kind from recipients of their bounty, whether as clients or as debtors. Unlike the rich, the openhearted farmers of Euboea did not "look for gifts in return."[5]

As the prophet Hermas's parable of the elm and the vine made plain, the gift of alms to the poor did not happen entirely without a return. But it was a deliberately inverted return. The solid gift of the hand was met by the ethereal (and for that reason incalculably valuable) gift of the mouth—by intercessory prayer for the rich offered to God by the poor. The imaginative logic that accompanied the joining of incommensurables—of earthly treasure to heaven, of rich to poor—was echoed in the spiritual exchange. The gift of material support was repaid by the immeasurable return of prayer and blessing.

This weight-free exchange avoided the sense of personal dependence which the patronage systems current in the Greco-Roman world forced upon the poor. If the Christian poor felt gratitude, this gratitude was not supposed to be directed to any individual donor. Rather, gratitude and a sense of obligation were to be reserved for God alone and for His church.

Christians were not alone in facing this issue. The "countercultural" implications of Jewish giving to the poor have recently been brought into sharp focus by Seth Schwartz in his study of Judaism at this time: *Were the Jews a Mediterranean Society? Reciprocity and Solidarity in Ancient Judaism*. This incisive book shows that the Jewish rabbis (though by no means necessarily the average Jews) were in the process of creating a countercultural code of giving to the poor that was quite as distinctive as that of the Christian communities. Schwartz's insights are particularly welcome because Christians of the second and third centuries frequently looked directly to their Jewish neighbors, or shared their concerns, at one remove, through the study of scriptures which they held in common with Jews. Both groups—rabbis and Christian leaders alike—were intensely concerned to maintain their reputation as "bearers of a potent and compelling counter culture."[6]

The rabbis went out of their way to ensure that gifts to the poor and to the rabbis (like gifts to the priests in the days of the Temple) did not carry the weight of obligation associated with normal gift giving. As interpreted by the rabbinic scholars of the second, third, and fourth centuries, "The Bible's elaborate rules [were] meant to ensure that the charitable donation (and likewise the donations meant to form the livelihood of the priestly and levitical temple staff) never degenerates into the dependency-generating gift."[7]

When it came to their own persons, and not just to the poor, the rabbis practiced with particular fierceness the countercultural rejection of the obligations usually created by the gift. They were expected to treat rich donors with calculated brusqueness: "For when he [the rich donor] benefits the rabbi, the rabbi becomes like clay."[8]

"Do This and Do It through the Bishop": From the *Didascalia Apostolorum* to Cyprian of Carthage

It is important to note the extent to which similar concerns to those of the rabbis ran through Christian writings of the same period. The Syriac *Didascalia Apostolorum* of around AD 220 was composed in the region outside Antioch. It was a frankly outré document. As its translator, Alistair Stewart-Sykes, points out, this book was a manual on "the control of donors." What was at stake was the "control . . . of funds through the control of people." It proposed the complete centralization of almsgiving in the hands of the bishop and his clergy.[9]

For this reason, the most thorough recent interpreter of the *Didascalia*, Georg Schöllgen, speaks with manifest misgiving about its "rigid clericalism."[10] According to the *Didascalia*, no laypersons were to give alms directly to the poor. Alms were to be brought first to the altar and then distributed by the bishop alone, through his priests and deacons. The poor who received these alms might be told the names of the donors. But they would be told in secret. In this way, the poor could offer intercessory prayer for their benefactors without publicizing their names in the community at large. By doing this, they avoided raising public esteem for individual rich givers. Secrecy also ensured that the poor did not mark themselves out in public as personally obligated to any particular donor.

The power of the prayers of the poor was treated as all the more effective for being hidden. Such prayers were the direct opposite to the traditional responses to the "dependency-generating gift." The poor were not to respond directly to the gifts of the rich. They were to be as silent and majestic as the altar. Like altars, the poor supported by the church were to be like places of

TREASURE IN HEAVEN

offering and prayer to God alone, untouched by earthly ties of gratitude to individual rich donors.[11]

The *Didascalia* proposed what, in many ways, was a utopian scheme. It demanded total anonymity on the part of the financial supporters of the church. But the scheme was devised so as to solve specific tensions. These tensions increasingly drove the Christian practice of almsgiving toward ever-greater centralization in the hands of clerical administrators. Only in this way could donors remain truly anonymous. "Do this and do it through the bishop" was the motto of the tract.[12]

This centralization invested the practice of religious giving with a sacral aura. But it was not only the bishop and clergy who gained from this process of sacralization. The quid pro quo of this seemingly high-handed arrangement was that if lay donors obeyed it, they could be certain that they had fulfilled the command of Jesus: *"lay up for yourselves treasure in heaven"* (Matt. 6:20).[13] In a situation of constant, increasingly sacralized giving, the sayings of Jesus on "treasure in heaven" imperceptibly merged with the idea of the treasures of the church. The two ideas were homologous: the idea of a distant treasure-house in heaven was echoed, on earth, by the idea of the church as possessing a sanctified treasure-house, as holy as that of any temple. By filling the treasuries of the church on a day-to-day basis, the incommensurable, invisible reward of treasure in heaven could be gained by members of the faithful without the total renunciation of all wealth.

I have lingered on the provisions of the *Didascalia Apostolorum* not because it was, in itself, a definitive document. Rather it represented an extreme statement of a trend in the finances of the Christian churches. In the course of the third century, bishops and clergy came to have greater control of the wealth donated by the laity. As Georg Schöllgen and others have made plain, the emergence of what we call a "monarchical episcopate" was intimately connected to the attempt of bishops to obtain a monopoly of church funds. Bishops began to act as the privileged distributors to the poor of the gifts of the laity.[14]

All that need be said of this development is that, in major

churches of the third century, it appears to have worked. The poor were fed and the clergy, who ministered to the poor, were increasingly honored by salaries raised in the same manner as alms were raised for the poor—through regular offerings by the laity. Bishops were proud of the financial muscle of their churches. Writing about a disputed election to the bishopric of Rome, in AD 251, Bishop Cornelius of Rome wrote to a colleague: "There can be only one bishop in a Catholic church in which . . . there are forty-six presbyters, seven deacons, seven sub-deacons, forty-two acolytes, readers and doorkeepers and more than fifteen hundred widows and distressed persons, all supported by the Lord's grace and love of humankind."[15]

These are the only statistics that we have for the finances of an early Christian church. They are impressive. It has been calculated that the clergy alone, along with their families, amounted to some six hundred persons.[16] The widows and distressed persons supported by the church were as numerous as all but the very largest trade association in the city.[17] Most important of all: when Cornelius spoke of "the Lord's grace and love of humankind," he referred to something precise. He meant that God, in His Providence, had endowed the church of Rome with an entire class of generous and willing donors, whose offerings supported these ambitious ventures.

Rome was not alone. As bishop of Carthage between 249 and 258, Cyprian showed what a bishop could do in a major Roman city.[18] On one occasion, he was able to gather one hundred thousand sesterces (the equivalent of a month's wages for three thousand workmen) through donations from the faithful, in order to ransom Christians taken captive in a raid by Berber tribesmen.[19] The original letter with which Cyprian announced this impressive levy was accompanied by a list of the donors for whom the communities should pray: "That you should be mindful of our brothers and sisters who have so promptly and willingly undertaken this very necessary work. May you thus ensure that they may never fail to do such works of mercy."[20]

Protected by the prayers of their fellow Christians, a wide constituency of lay donors were plainly encouraged to remain prosperous so that they could remain generous. The historian wishes that this list had survived. It might have provided what we dearly need: a social profile of a rich Christian church in a major city on the eve of the full onset of the empirewide crisis of the third century. For such persons, to place *treasure in heaven* was not to abandon their wealth, but to keep it so as to give constant financial aid to the church.[21]

Ordo-Building: The Church on the Eve of the Great Persecution (AD 303)

But it was never simply a matter of financial resources. The clergy did not only receive salaries. They also received honor. They sat while others stood. At banquets, they received larger helpings.[22] Altogether, all over the Mediterranean, the Christian churches joined with gusto in what Onno van Nijf (in his study of the professional associations of the Greek East in this period) has called the process of "*ordo*-building"—the replication, in miniature, by groups of artisans and tradesfolk, of the solemn order of the upper-class city council.[23] In becoming city councils in miniature, these little groups became fully paid up participants in what John Lendon has called the "empire of honor."[24] With their hierarchy of offices and their complicated rules for procedure and membership, the associations were marked out as the gathering points of "honorable" persons.

Among Christians also, *ordo*-building had come to stay. Indeed, it had come to stay with such gusto that the local churches seemed to many pious observers to have come to replicate the extremes associated with the politics of town councils and trade associations in the secular world. Episcopal elections were the occasion for vigorous canvassing. The clergy took bribes. Bishops curried favor with rich donors. Viewing the state of Christianity in around AD 240, the great Origen of Alexandria (ca. 185–254) wrote that if Christ were to return to earth to witness the behavior of the modern laity and clergy, he would have wept over the church as he had once wept over the sinful city of Jerusalem.[25] Deeply distressing to persons such as Origen, these abuses showed that Christianity had come to stay in the cities of the empire.

For this reason, it is not surprising that when the Great Persecution erupted under the emperor Diocletian, in 303, it was as a series of little *ordines*, and not as a scatter of individuals, that Christianity was attacked. Each local church was an *ordo* of its own. Each had its bishop and clergy, and each had its own resources: buildings, scriptures, sacred vessels, and supplies for the poor. These could be considerable. When Bishop Mensurius of Carthage was summoned to the imperial court in 308, "the congregation was greatly distressed because the church had a great many ornaments of gold and silver which it could not bury in the ground or carry away. He entrusted these to faithful leading laymen [*seniores*] making an inventory which he was said to have given to a certain old lady."[26]

Once again, as with Cyprian and his list of donors, the historian wishes that this inventory had survived. But we know that the amount hidden was sufficient for the *seniores* of the church of Carthage to renege on their promise to return the wealth of the church to the next bishop. They established a church of their own, thereby originating what came to be known as the Donatist Schism. Or so we are told by their enemies. Even if the accusation was false, it showed that the wealth of the church of Carthage, in gold and silver plate alone, was considered worth fighting for.[27]

Provincial churches were no less wealthy. In 303, the local authorities charged with the task of confiscating church property found what is, for us, precious evidence of what "business as usual" had meant for a Christian church of the late third century. At Cirta (modern Constantine, in Algeria) they made straight for the warehouse of the church. There they found "2 gold chalices, 6 silver chalices, 6 silver urns, a silver cooking pot, [along with 22 candlesticks and hanging lamps; and] 87 women's tunics, 38 capes, 16 men's tunics, 13 pairs of men's shoes, 47 pairs of women's shoes, and 19 *coplae* [possibly cloak clasps or brooches]." But what the commissioners at Cirta had also come for were books (especially the Christian scriptures), to be impounded and burned. Searches in the church and from house to house revealed an impressive number of books: "one extremely large *codex*"; four from one house, five from another, eight from another, five large and two small codices from yet another.[28]

An Age of Teachers

This impressive haul of books brings us to the end of our chapter. To devote exclusive attention (as many sociological studies of early Christianity have done) to the structural problems within the Christian community that accompanied the rise of a unitary episcopate and a professionalized clergy is to tell only half the story. It is not so much to miss the forest for the trees. Rather, it is to miss the sap in the trees themselves. We must never overlook the sheer zest that average persons in the late classical period (in the second and third centuries AD)—pagans, Jews, and Christians alike—put into the pursuit of religion. This pursuit of religion was not driven by an ill-defined religious fervor. It expressed an intellectual hunger—a hunger to understand things divine—whose power and widespread nature have come as a surprise to historians of the late classical world.

As in the England of the Victorian age (after the urbane incredulity of the eighteenth century), so in the Roman Empire of the second and third centuries AD, it became exciting to talk about religion. But, by the third century AD, not only did many persons wish to talk about religion. There were also many religious groups (and not least the Christians) who had developed systems of financial support that left increasing numbers of persons (many of whom did not come from the leisured upper classes) free to talk about religion all the time.

It is not easy to explain this change of mood. Some scholars, notably John North, have suggested that the development of a "marketplace of religions" had come to replace the traditional monopoly of cults upheld by the upper classes.[29] Others have stressed the greater horizontal mobility of cults that had been fostered by the commercial unity of the Roman world.[30] In fact, no single factor seems to account for the somewhat random scatter of Christian communities at this time.[31]

But at least the change of mood itself can be delineated more sharply than has been done in the scholarship of previous generations. We are not dealing with an "Age of Anxiety"—to use the title of E. R. Dodds's haunting (but outdated) description of religious experience in the age between Marcus Aurelius and Constantine.[32] We are dealing, rather, with an Age of Questioning—with the flowering of a novel intellectualism devoted to religious topics. In a brilliant chapter in the joint book of Jean-Michel Carrié and Aline Rousselle, *L'empire romain en mutation des Sévères à Constantin*, Rousselle characterizes this new attitude to religion. She speaks of a drive toward *l'explicitation du croire*—a growing sense of the need to unravel and explain the content of religions and of their attendant practices. This novel religious intellectualism was not limited to new religions, such as Christianity. Upholders of traditional cults were also touched by "a powerful need to justify and to explain" practices which they had previously taken for granted.[33]

We should not underestimate the number and the social spread of persons who asked for explanations. If we do overlook this phenomenon it is because we are committed to an impoverished view of the complexity of Roman society in the second and third centuries. We tend to underrate the speed with which ideas circulated within the Roman Empire and the social range of persons affected by them.

We do this because we have been misled by two, mutually reinforcing stereotypes. On one hand, as we have seen, for members of the educated upper classes (even for Christian bishops such as Gregory of Nyssa), the idea that persons tainted by labor could indulge in intellectual activity seemed absurd. On the other hand, Christians often defined themselves against their fellow intellectuals among the subelites by contrasting the simplicity of the Christian faith with the willful complexity and elitism of pagan thinkers. The "rhetoric of paradox" by which Christians exalted the spiritual power of their humble religion over against the empty wisdom of the "world" has tended to mislead us into taking this pose at face value.[34]

Christians frequently boasted of their outreach to the unedu-

TREASURE IN HEAVEN

cated. They claimed that Christianity offered "Philosophy for Dummies." Its doctrines were accessible to the masses. In the words of Alexander of Lycopolis, a Platonic philosopher from Egypt, disputing the religious system of the Manichees around AD 300: "This was, I believe, correctly understood by Jesus, and this is why, in order that farmers and carpenters and masons and other skilled workers should not be excluded from the good, he instituted a common circle of all these people together . . . and by means of simple and easy teach-ins, he led them towards an understanding of God and helped them to achieve their desire for the good."[35]

However, both stereotypes are profoundly misleading. The elite culture of the empire was never as hermetically sealed against outsiders as those who upheld this culture wished to believe. Nor, despite their professions of humility, were the Christians an uneducated group, devoid of intellectual curiosity.

Both stereotypes have been accepted largely without challenge for a further reason. Our image of Roman society as a whole has unduly stressed the chasm between rich and poor, and hence between upper- and lower-class culture. As a result of such a polarized view, we have tended to pay less attention to intermediate layers of society, and to the wide variety of social niches in which cultural activity took place.[36] We suffer from what Walter Scheidel has acutely called "binary tunnel vision."[37] We see only a world rigidly divided between the leisured upper classes and the poor. As a result, we miss the sheer zest with which wide sections of Roman society, well below the level of the elites, threw themselves into the business of making sense of the world in religious terms.

Nor should we underestimate the vigor and ingenuity of those who offered solutions to religious problems. To take one example: The recent work of Roger Beck on Mithraism reveals the energy with which relatively humble, even stodgy persons "labored in their minds" to create an entirely new religion.[38] Yet, as Beck points out, the "burst of inventiveness" associated with the elaboration of the mysteries of Mithras has passed largely unnoticed among scholars of the ancient world.[39] Because it spread, in

Beck's sharp words, among "antiquity's non-chattering classes" the study of Mithraism has had to overcome "an ingrained bias against allowing that anything of intellectual worth might grow independently of the traditions of the elite."[40]

Yet, religious thought happened. So did religious teaching. Among the images found on an early second-century Mithraic cup recently discovered at Mainz, the figure of the Mystagogue is shown with the simple robe and upraised arm of a rhetor and teacher.[41] In late antiquity, such figures came into their own all over the Mediterranean and the Middle East—and not least among the Christians.

Christians, indeed, shared the zest for teaching to a marked degree. Third-century papyri from Egypt, now interpreted by AnneMarie Luijendijk in her book *"Greetings in the Lord": Early Christians and the Oxyrhynchus Papyri*, show that many Christians took their catechesis seriously. Bishops wrote letters introducing catechumens who had traveled in Egypt in search of *oikodomé*—spiritual edification. These catechumens were categorized according to the books of the Bible that they were in the process of mastering—some were on Genesis, some were on the Gospel of John.[42]

As a result, every major Christian community had its equivalent of a think tank. And the greatest think tank of all, of course, was that which came to gravitate around the mighty Origen. From 234 to his death in 254, Origen taught at Caesarea Maritima (in modern Israel). He collected a stupendous library. In the words of Tony Grafton and Megan Williams, in their recent study *Christianity and the Transformation of the Book*, this library was "one of the greatest single monuments of Roman scholarship."[43]

Such scholarship did not happen for nothing. As a result, Christian teachers such as Origen found themselves asking much the same questions about the nature of their financial support as did the rabbis and the Christian clergy. Only the most rich among them could afford to "go it alone" with a private library and the immense staff of copyists and book producers that were needed for scholarly ventures in the ancient world. Christian teachers were not rich to that extent. Rather, they found them-

TREASURE IN HEAVEN

selves constantly exposed, as the rabbis and the Christian clergy had been exposed, to the dangers of the "dependency-generating gift."

Origen faced this issue throughout his life. He had begun his career as the protégé of Ambrosios, a rich bureaucrat. He had even replaced a teacher of Valentinian Gnosis who had been Ambrosios's previous guru. As a patron, Ambrosios did him proud: "Shorthand writers more than seven in number were available when he dictated, relieving each other regularly, and at least as many copyists, as well as girls trained in penmanship."[44]

Though Origen had originally been aided by Ambrosios as an individual patron, the study circle that grew up around him at Caesarea Maritima was an even more ambitious venture. Christoph Markschies has rightly called it "the first Christian private university to appear in the ancient world."[45] It was probably supported by donations from visiting students. It may also have been partly funded by the local church.

Origen's library was a stupendous affair. It comprised, among other marvels, eight hundred works of the master and forty vast tomes of his famous *Hexapla*—variant translations of the complete Old Testament set beside the Hebrew in six columns. Within a generation of his death, this library had become part of the church of Caesarea.[46] It would have been supported by the pious giving of the local congregation much as the bishop and clergy were supported. Altogether, Origen was an outstanding example of a *Chalcenteros*, a "brazen-bowelled" intellectual, set free to study and teach by the labors of others. This support enabled Origen to emerge as "the first fully professional Christian thinker."[47]

Freelance intellectuals caused trouble to the local clergy from time to time. But, despite these problems, it was well worth the expense for a major church to support them. They buttressed the faith. We should have no illusions about the aim of this intense teaching activity, whether among pagans, Christians, or Jews. It was not to allow free range to the mind, as modern persons might wish it to have been. Far from it. Late antique philosophers were there to teach the art of certainty. Their intellectual program was dominated by the need to remove doubt. They expected their students to find their way to absolute truth and to cling to it all the more fiercely for having resolved the intellectual problems and banished the misconceptions that stood in the way of total commitment. For only then would the student be set free from error so as to become a new person.[48] Intellectual activity of this kind braced the church, as the bearer of total truth, against the errors of the world.[49]

One need only look at fourth-century representations of Christ as a teacher surrounded by his Apostles to sense the urgency—and the hard edges—of this widespread drive to understand so as to banish doubt. In the words of Paul Zanker, in his memorable book *The Mask of Socrates: The Image of the Intellectual in Antiquity*, "For the first time we are confronted with a clearly defined hierarchy, in which the teacher enjoys absolute authority, and the pupil appears fully devoted to him. Furthermore, for the first time, the viewer is addressed directly. . . . [We are] drawn into the group receiving instruction, yet at the same time distanced by a sense of awe."[50]

As we will see, the fourth century would have its fair share of awe-inspiring teachers. We often fail to recognize many of them because they came to bear the newly coined name of "monks."[51] But we should not be misled by the apparent novelty of this Christian buzzword. The "monks" of Syria and Egypt, exotic though they might seem at first sight, did not mark an entirely new departure. Many of them played a role within the Christian community that had long been prepared through the religious questioning of the second and third centuries. In many cases, scholarly monks merely replaced monk-like scholars, such as Origen, as teachers and spiritual guides.[52]

Furthermore, the financial resources for the support of such persons were now in place. Alongside the ordinary poor, striking figures of the "holy poor" (administrators, teachers, and individual exemplars of heroic virtue—would-be martyrs, ascetics, and virgins) had already established a claim on the pockets of the faithful. They were the beneficiaries of the tension between the "real" poor and the "holy poor" that we have traced since the days of Saint Paul.

So let us turn, in our next chapter, to the extreme eastern edge of the Christian world of the late third century—to Syria and Mesopotamia. There we will meet the most radical teacher of all—the prophet Mani. Mani was a younger contemporary of Origen. He also knew how to remove doubt. The Coptic translation of a massive, thousand-page exposé of Mani's ideas was simply called the *Kephalaia [the Chapters] of The Teacher.* Mani was, above all, known as "The Teacher." In every *kephalaion*—in every chapter—of this great tome, Mani, as The Teacher, resolved a religious problem posed to him by his disciples. "The Teacher said . . ." was the constant refrain of the book.[53] From the late third century onward, the "Holy Church" of Mani and his followers, known as Manichaeans or Manichees, would dog the Christian churches of the Mediterranean and the Middle East as a doppelgänger to themselves—alternately horrifying and alluring.

Furthermore, the leaders of the "Holy Church" of Mani, the Elect, were financed by the rank and file of the church in a manner that took to a new high pitch the notion of the joining of heaven to earth through the flow of alms to the "holy poor." Never before had the theme of alms to *the poor among the saints* been presented in so radical a manner, both by members of the Manichaean Elect and (as we shall see) by many other Christian ascetics in Syria. These "holy poor" stood out as persons who had abandoned labor. They were supported by the alms of their fellow believers. Not surprisingly, therefore, their activities prompted lively debates on labor that touched on the very foundations of human society and on its relation to the natural world. It is to these persons and to these debates that we will turn in our next chapters.

3

"The Treasuries That Are in the Heights": The Elect, the Catechumens, and the Cosmos in Manichaeism

The "Holy Poor" and the Spiritual Exchange

In my last two chapters, I traced a tension in the Christian practice of religious giving. On the one hand, there was the primordial command of Jesus to his disciples: *"Sell your possessions and give alms; provide yourselves with purses that do not grow old, with a treasure in the heavens that does not fail, where no thief approaches and no moth destroys"* (Luke 12:33). On the other hand, there was the notion of the spiritual exchange. This notion was expressed most clearly in a letter of Saint Paul. Writing to the Christian community in Corinth, Paul summed up the claims for financial support of "apostles" and of similar religious leaders in a powerful image: *"If we have sown spiritual good among you, is it too much to reap your material benefits?"* (1 Cor. 9:11).

By the year AD 300, the notion of a spiritual exchange was ensconced in the Christian imagination. Only a few might follow the call of Jesus to *"sell all . . . and come, follow me"* (Matt. 19:21). But any Christian could reach out to touch heaven itself through entering into a regular exchange of material support in return for blessing, initiation, and teaching offered by Christians who lived from the wealth of others. They were the "holy poor" of the Christian community.

These members of the "holy poor" varied greatly. They included bishops and a newly professionalized clergy. The process of giving to the bishop (and especially of giving to the poor through the bishop) was increasingly sacralized. Bishops and clergy came to be spoken of as "Levites." They were likened to the priests of ancient Israel.

This title did not only serve to surround them with an ancient, sacral aura. The phrase was also used to pinpoint the unusual nature of their wealth. In Old Testament times, the Levites had enjoyed a peculiar position in Israelite society. They owned no land. Instead, they were fed from the gifts of those who owned and worked the land. (One must add that their dependence on the yield of every harvest for their own living ensured that they celebrated with due promptness the rites that they were expected to perform for the fertility of the land!) In theory at least, bishops and clergy were the Levites of the new Christian age. In the well-chosen words of Seth Schwartz, they were to be "a class of functionaries or enablers, suspended between privilege and pauperdom."[1]

Bishops and clergy, therefore, could be treated like the Levites of old. They were to remain poor in the midst of wealth. But, by the year AD 300, there were other, more glamorous figures who claimed to be members of the "holy poor." They were not mere administrators of wealth. They depended directly on the wealth of others. They were partners in a spiritual exchange by which material support was repaid by spiritual blessing.

These "holy poor" increasingly included exemplars of ascetic virtue. In the words of a dramatic third-century legend, the *Acts of Judas Thomas:* good Christians, of course, were expected to give to the poor; but they were expected to give "particularly [*malista*] to those who live in a state of holiness [having renounced wealth and sex]."[2] The *Acts of Judas Thomas* were written in ascetic circles in Syria. These circles already took a binary model of the Christian community for granted. In every church, average Christians were supposed to support a privileged group of the "holy poor."

"Let Them Be Esteemed by You as God upon Earth"

We should not underestimate the strength of this current in the Christianity of the late third century. Nor was the wish for contact with holy figures limited to Christians. We need only turn back to Lucian to realize the power of this yearning for a touch of the divine on earth. As we have seen, as a satirist, Lucian was quite prepared to place the flamboyant religious leaders of his time in a second-century equivalent of "Pseuds Corner." But he made an exception for his own hero, the Cynic sage Demonax:

He lived almost a hundred years, without illness or pain, bothering nobody and asking nothing of anyone. Not only Athenians but all Greece conceived such affection for him that, when he passed by, the magistrates rose up in his honor and there was silence everywhere. Towards the end, when he was very old, he used to eat and sleep uninvited in any house which he chanced to be passing, and the inmates thought that it was almost like the epiphany of a god, and that a benign guardian spirit had entered their house.[3]

Fiercely self-supporting, as a proper Cynic was expected to be, Lucian's Demonax did not seek financial support. He had no wish to be a partner in a high-pitched "spiritual exchange." But with Christians it was different. They wanted to support their heroes. To do so was to turn "treasure on earth" into "treasure in heaven." Lucian's account of the time spent by his bugbear Peregrinus among the Christians showed this clearly. When in prison, Peregrinus was showered with food and gifts from the local Christian community.

The Christian treatment of Peregrinus was not exceptional. Already in the second century AD, potential Christian martyrs in prison (the "confessors") received the same intense reverence from Christian congregations as holy men and women would do in later times. Though deeply suspicious of fly-by-night "prophets," the author of the *Didascalia Apostolorum* urged local Christians to spare no pains in visiting and feeding confessors of the faith (potential martyrs) in prison: "Let them be esteemed by you . . . as God upon earth. For through them you see the Lord our Savior."[4]

In this chapter, I will examine one radical group that emerged principally in Syria in the late third century. This group was committed to an exceptionally high-pitched version of the spiritual exchange between its leaders and the rank and file. These were

TREASURE IN HEAVEN

the followers of Mani. They were called Manichaeans or Manichees. But the Manichees were not alone. They formed part of what might be called a Christian "radical consensus." They shared with other radical Syrian Christians a distinctive way of life, in communities structured in a distinctive manner. These Christian ascetics claimed to be living a life "in the likeness of the angels." Like angels, they did not work. They expected to be supported by the faithful as part of a spiritual exchange.

"The Grand Junction": Syria

In order to follow these two groups (the Manichaean and the non-Manichaean ascetics of Syria), we must go to the crucial region where the Fertile Crescent joined Mesopotamia to the Mediterranean in a great northern arc that stretched from Iraq, through Syria, to Antioch and then southward to the boundaries of Egypt. This area was known to Greeks and Romans as Syria, or more generally as "the East."

At the time, "Syria" was a vaguer term than it is today. It covered many Roman provinces. It spread from Iraq into modern eastern Turkey, and reached as far south as modern Israel, Palestine, and Jordan. Readers will have to make a mental adjustment to their map of the modern Middle East so as to think of ancient Syria as a region that was more extensive than the frontiers of the modern state of Syria.

They should not think of Syria as a homogeneous region. In the trenchant words of Christian Sahner's recent book on the past and present of Syria: "Far from being a geographic and cultural unit [Syria, in the ancient, wider sense] is actually a patchwork of fragmented landscapes, from the rugged valleys of Lebanon to the flowing grainfields of Palestine, and from the arid expanses of the Eastern Desert to the lunar crags of southern Jordan."[5]

But it was precisely the diversity of the Syrian landscape that accounts for its distinctiveness. In antiquity, these many "subclimates" were held together by constant trade and by frequent cultural interchanges. The need for communication favored the emergence of various forms of lingua franca. In this period, a form of Aramaic centered on Edessa won out as a literary language in most regions (but not in Aramaic Palestine). This is what we now call Syriac. But Greek also formed a lingua franca in the western parts of Syria. As a result, bilingualism—in Greek and Syriac—was the norm in much of Syria. Altogether, it was a region characterized by a remarkable degree of cultural and linguistic interconnectivity.

We should think, in particular, of northern Syria (between Antioch and Mesopotamia) as a corridor—as a great chain of intensely worked settlements (villages as much as towns) that ran from the Euphrates to the Mediterranean along the foothills of what are now northern Iraq, northern Syria, and southeastern Turkey. It is largely this northern corridor that we will focus on in this and the next chapter. For this area was the keystone of the great arch of the Fertile Crescent.

Syria bridged two worlds. In the words of Martin West, ever since the second millennium BC, Syria had been "the grand junction" that linked Asia to the Mediterranean.[6] This remained the case in our period. Speaking of the art and architecture of the region in Roman and late Roman times, the archaeologist John Ward-Perkins has made plain that "the frontier territory between Rome and Parthia [the Persian Empire] was neither a cultural barrier nor a mere gateway and point of passage between East and West. It was a vital creative center in its own right, and it was this fact above all which enabled it to serve as an effective intermediary between two great civilizations which flourished on its borders."[7]

Already in the middle and late third century, this crucial region was crisscrossed by religious groups of Christian origin. Many of these groups were content to form settled Christian communities in cities and villages. But others were distinguished by an "apostolic" mobility. They combined the missionary universalism of Saint Paul with the ideal of wandering poverty associated with the disciples of Jesus in the Gospels. They were a sight to be seen. The author of a letter written to direct the behavior of such groups warned them that when they passed through pagan villages, they should not burst out into singing the Psalms (which they usually did, so as to hearten the local Christians), lest they be mistaken for a troupe of traveling musicians![8]

These wanderers were local products. They were not a new phenomenon in Syria. Throughout the classical period, the great sanctuary of the goddess Atargatis at Hierapolis/Bambyke (modern Membidj, Syria)—on the busy road that led from the Euphrates to Aleppo—would send out crowds of begging priests known as *agyrtai*, sacred beggars. Carrying with them the curse or blessing of a powerful goddess, the *agyrtai* brought back sacks full of coins. In the second century AD, one such beggar-priest collected forty sacks in twenty journeys, with which he set up a votive statue to the goddess at Kfar Haoura in the hills of northern Lebanon.[9]

Other holy mendicants may have come from yet farther east. It is possible that Buddhist monks had settlements in southern Mesopotamia, at the head of the Persian Gulf. The doctrines of yet more radical wanderers, the Jains of the Deccan, may also have been known.[10]

Not all these wanderers were long-distance travelers. Nor were they always in constant motion. Their notion of "wandering" was rather different from ours. As in Buddhism, wandering expressed a profound indifference to the world in which they found themselves. They were "strangers." Every place was equal because equally foreign to them.

This meant, in practice, that these holy "wanderers" showed a disturbing ability to cross boundaries that seemed rigid to normal persons. They could join the desert to the city, the open road to the villages. When they settled, they chose, by preference, to settle in nonplaces—in caves, in the bottoms of empty cisterns, on top of columns, and even in the branches of trees.[11] But they did so in the middle of populous and prosperous regions. It was as "strangers" in this sense that they came to permeate the landscape of the Fertile Crescent—towns, villages, hilltops, steppe lands, and all.

These Christian wanderers had a long tradition behind them. Many scholars have wished to see in them a form of Christian religious life that reached back directly to the "wandering charismatics" of Gospel times.[12] They argue that the Aramaic-speaking world of Syria as a whole had remained closer (both socially and religiously) to the Galilee of Jesus of Nazareth and his disciples than was the urban Christianity of the Greco-Roman Mediterranean. Whatever we may think of this claim to be part of some primordial Christianity, the activities of these wanderers were plain for all to see by AD 300. They were made possible by a pattern of relations between themselves and the average believers that was already firmly in place. They expected to be supported entirely by the alms of those to whom they ministered.

Toward the end of the third century, the wanderers of Syria were joined by missionaries from yet farther to the East, from central Mesopotamia (to the south of the Persian capital at Ctesiphon). These were the messengers of a new prophet, Mani. Mani had died as a martyr at the hands of the Sasanian King of Kings, in 277. He saw himself as the Paul of his age. He was believed to have sent his emissaries as "Apostles," to establish his "Holy Church" in all regions of the earth—from the Roman Empire in the West to the Kushan kingdom of Central Asia in the East. Mani's missionaries came to be called the "Elect" of his church. Following current Christian practice, those to whom they ministered were called *catechumens* or, in the Latin West, *Auditores*—"Hearers."[13]

The Elect claimed to model their behavior on exactly the same pattern of extreme poverty combined with ceaseless mobility which radical Christians in Syria had come to see as the distinctive mark of all true disciples of Jesus. The words of the great Manichaean Coptic Psalms of the Wanderers echo scenarios taken from the Gospels and from the Apocryphal Acts of the Apostles:

> They went from village to village.
> [They] went into the roads hungry, with no bread in their
>   hands.

They walked in the heat, thirsting, they took no water to drink.
No gold, no silver, no money, did they take with them on
their way.
They went into the villages, not knowing anybody. They were
welcomed for His sake, they were loved for His name's sake.[14]

The Manichaean movement faced both east and west. Mani
had developed his message in Persian-controlled Mesopotamia. He was believed to have established relations with the new
Sasanian dynasty, and especially with the great King of Kings,
Shapur I (240–72). His missionary journeys may have taken him
throughout Iran as far as the borders of Central Asia in the north
and India in the south. Unfortunately, the Mesopotamian and
Iranian dimensions of the life and preaching of Mani are largely
lost to us.[15] What we know far better is the Manichaeism of the
West. This was a Manichaeism rooted in Syrian forms of radical
Christianity.

Mani probably felt most at home in this Syrian world. He had
grown up on the easternmost fringe of the Aramaic-speaking
world, where Syriac had begun to emerge as a major literary language. This world stretched, without a break, from the Zagros
Mountains to the Mediterranean. All but one of Mani's works
were originally written in Syriac. This was the face that his religion showed to the western Christian world. It was far from
exotic. To most Christian communities in Syria, the Manichaean
missionaries came, simply, as avatars of Saint Paul and of the
Apostles as these figures were imagined by Christian believers of
the third century.

"The Treasuries That Are in the Heights":
Elect and Catechumens

It was as travelers from Syria that the followers of Mani first entered the Nile valley. We must remember that it is merely an
accident of preservation, due to the bone-dry sands of Egypt,
which has ensured that the bulk of the original documents of the
Manichaean movement have survived in Egypt on papyrus, in

the form of letters and of translations from Syriac into Greek and Coptic. What we now have are no more than the scattered remnants, in translation, of one of the greatest outbursts of religious creativity yet to emerge from the Syriac-speaking world.

Major Manichaean texts in Coptic were found, in 1930, in the Fayyum—an oasis close to the Nile delta. In 1990 yet more (both in Greek and Coptic) were discovered far to the south, at Ismant al-Kharab (ancient Kellis) in the Dakhlah oasis in the western desert of Egypt.[16] It is to these last that I will turn. Through these documents, we have access to outposts of the Manichaean movement that were placed some 2,000 miles away from the original home of Mani, in central Iraq.

Kellis lay over 750 miles to the south of Alexandria. A cache of Manichaean letters, dating perhaps from the 340s, were discovered, in 1990, in the corner of one house. They enable us, for the very first time, to listen to a Manichaean community from the inside. And what we overhear is a markedly Christian religious language. In the words of their first editor, Iain Gardner, Manichaeism in Kellis could be "best described as a superior and more effective form of Christianity."[17] Indeed, in the minds of its adherents, Manichaeism was, quite simply, "*the* authentic Christianity."[18]

One letter is addressed to the Lady Eirene, a catechumen—a lay disciple of the Manichaean Elect. In this letter, a member of the Elect praised Eirene for having placed her treasure in heaven in the right way. She had offered material support to the Elect:

> She whose deeds resemble her name [Peace], our [spiritual] daughter . . . the daughter of the holy church; the catechumen of the faith; the good tree whose fruit never withers, which is your love which emits radiance every day. She who has acquired for herself her riches and stored them away in the *treasuries that are in the heights, where moths shall not find a way nor shall thieves dig through to them to steal.*[19]

The last lines are a direct citation from the Gospel of Luke, with which we began this chapter. But the letter then added an explanation of the *treasuries that are in the heights:* "which [trea-

TREASURE IN HEAVEN

suries] are the Sun and the Moon."[20] It was only this last, telltale reference to the Sun and the Moon as active agents in a cosmic drama of salvation which identified the writer of the letter as a Manichee. But the notion of placing treasure in heaven through giving to the poor was common to both Judaism and Christianity.

This newly discovered exchange of Manichaean letters shows, with the crispness of an X-ray photograph, one path by which "treasure on earth" was believed to flow directly upward to become "treasure in heaven." Let us look at this more closely.

First: the Elect needed Eirene and her fellow catechumens:

> You being for us helpers and worthy patrons and firm unbending pillars [of the church; cf. Gal. 2:9]; while we ourselves rely upon you. . . . I was very grateful to you, ten million times! [Whether] we are far or [we are near]; indeed, we have found remembrance among [you]. Now, therefore, may it stay with you: this Knowledge and this Faith [which you have] known and believed in. Therefore, [I] beg you, [my] blessed [daughters], that you will [send] me two *choes* of oil. For [you] know yourselves that we are [in need] here; since we are afflicted.[21]

It was a very oily letter.

But, second: what did Eirene gain from her gift? She gained teaching, intercession, and, ultimately, salvation. At the time of her death, she could hope that the rituals and prayers performed by the Elect would help her soul to ascend peacefully to heaven, protected from the "thousand afflictions" that lurked in the other world.[22]

The interdependence of Elect and catechumens was common to all Manichaean communities wherever they were. It is most clearly stated in a unique Manichaean document that was discovered in 1918 in a dry cave in North Africa, outside Theveste (modern Tebessa in Algeria). It may have been written at the same time when the young Augustine, as an *Auditor*—a "Hearer," a catechumen—of the Manichees (in the 370s), was solemnly bringing food to the Elect in return for their mighty prayers.[23]

Known to scholars as the Codex Thevestinus, this treatise of twenty-six parchment leaves spelled out the duty of the Hearers to support the Elect. It was made up of a patchwork of citations from the Gospels and from the letters of Saint Paul. These citations dealt with exactly the same issues that we have touched upon in our last two chapters. For the writer, the Pauline citations proved that "these two ranks, founded on the same faith in the same church, support one another. Each gives to the other from their abundant possessions, the Elect to the hearers from their heavenly treasure . . . and the hearers to the elect from their earthly treasure."[24]

In the words of a recent, lucid summary of the Manichaean system: "The establishment of this bicameral (two-fold) structure was regarded by the Manichaeans themselves as the major institutional achievement of the Manichaean church."[25] But, as we have seen, the Manichaean "bicameral" division between Elect and catechumens was no more than a final, radical version of the well-established Christian tendency to create some form of "spiritual exchange" between the laity and holy persons. What made the Manichees different was that the spiritual exchange on which their bicameral system was based had no room in it for the real poor. Alms were for the "holy" poor—the Elect—alone.

Cosmos and Society in Manichaeism

Contemporary Christians savagely attacked the Manichaeans for their apparent heartlessness in ignoring the poor.[26] Although giving to the "holy poor" and the church were encouraged (and often fervently practiced) in Christian circles, this never took place to the exclusion of the poor. The basic rule was clear. Christians were almsgivers. Those who did not give alms to the poor could not be saved.

As a result, Christian almsgiving was supposed to bring real benefits to real persons in a real society. With the Manichees, by contrast, the poor—and, with the poor, society itself—became transparent. Manichaean catechumens looked through them. Only the austere Elect counted for them as proper recipients of alms. For only the ethereal prayers of the Elect could save their souls.

An entire view of the universe lay behind this extreme option. Put very briefly: among the Manichees, the nature of the material world itself was at stake. It was their bleak view of the cosmos as a whole that gave a sharp flavor to their notion of almsgiving to the "holy poor" alone. A Manichaean catechumen, such as the Lady Eirene, believed that nothing she could do to help the poor would save her soul. For her soul was trapped in a catastrophe of cosmic proportions from which only the prayers of the Elect could deliver her. Only the "holy poor"—the Elect, with their powerful prayers and unearthly lifestyle—could ensure that her *earthly treasure* would come to rest in "the treasuries that are in the heights," and that her soul would eventually follow that treasure to heaven.[27]

In this, the Manichees differed markedly from other Christians. Following a tradition shared with Judaism, Christians had tended to believe that wealth itself was somehow touched by the providence of God. By giving to the church and to the poor, the pious Christian gave back to God a little of the abundance of a created world shot through with His blessing.[28] In a similar way, the Eucharist was presented as a return to God of His good gifts. The bread and wine brought to the altar were spoken of as "these Thy gifts and creatures of bread and wine."[29]

Such prayers assumed a basically sunny view of the natural world as the good creation of God. This view of the natural world spilled over easily into an equally sunny view of the wealth that was taken from the natural world. Wealth also enjoyed God's blessing. It had been given by God to believers so that they could give back to Him a part of it, in the form of donations to the church, to holy persons, and to the poor. By the end of the third century, both synagogues and churches were described as having been funded "from the gifts of the providence of God."[30]

But no Manichee could possibly harbor such comfortable illusions about the material world. Wine, they knew, was not a "gift of God." It was not even a "creature of God." It was the poisonous blood of wounded demons, mixed deep into matter, and liable to erupt in the dangerous fruit of the vine.[31] The best that could be said of the material universe was that it was (in the words of a later, Chinese catechism of the Manichaean faith) an immense distillery. It was like one of those magical laboratories in which alchemists had sought, through a prolonged process of refinement, to wrench from base matter, in minute, ethereal fragments, the unalloyed essence of gold and of similar time-defying substances.[32]

It is against this cosmic backdrop that we should place the ritual support offered by the Manichaean catechumens to their Elect. The "wealth" that they offered to the Elect was not a representative portion of the goodness of a material world, created by God and gladly offered back to Him by the faithful. It was a last, thin vestige of matter, painstakingly prized loose from an inherently evil world, and sent on its way (in the form of a solemn gift of sustenance to the Elect) toward some final transmutation in "the treasuries in the heights." Such wealth, offered in this way, was believed to carry with it the very souls of its donors.[33]

For this was wealth from which the demonic energy of process had been drained. It was wealth "laid to rest." The Coptic term, *mton*, usually translated as "rest," is crucial to the Manichaean view of the material world.[34] The food offered to the Elect had been detached from the sinister exuberance of the vegetable world, through plucking (in the case of fruit, a favored food of the Elect) or through being cut by the sickle. Lying on a dish, a true *nature morte* detached from nature, this was food through which the negative current of energy associated with demonic "matter" no longer pulsed.[35]

This food was offered to those whose entire life, also, had come to a stop. The Elect were "sealed" on their mouths, their hands, and their genitals.[36] They were thus sealed off from process. They did not join themselves to fully "living" matter through unregulated eating. They did not contribute to the headlong pullulation of human flesh through intercourse and the begetting of children. Above all, they did not lend their hands to manual labor in the fields. For by stooping to work, they would have involved themselves in the most bloody process of all—the tearing of the earth through plowing and through the slashing of living vegetation.[37] With pale faces and soft, white hands,

TREASURE IN HEAVEN

the Elect—men and women alike, for, in this, they were indistinguishable—had left "the world." They already lived on the threshold of the mighty "cessation" that would eventually fall upon the cosmos as a whole.

Such a view had palpable social implications. For Mani and his disciples, the social world was dwarfed by a towering cosmos. The relative distribution of wealth and poverty in society lacked positive meaning. No hint of the providence of God could be seen in it. The division between rich and poor was just one of the many ugly accidents that occurred in a material universe stirred at random by the influence of demonic planetary "lords."[38] In such a worldview, wealth could never be called "a gift of the providence of God," given to the rich by God so that they could give alms to the poor.

For this reason, labor, the world of drudgery—of *ponos*—was treated by the Manichaean Elect as a peculiarly charged emblem of bondage to the world of matter. Catechumens might work the fields.[39] The Elect could never do this. For the Elect, to hold oneself back from labor was to draw a clear line between oneself and the endless turning of a sinister cosmic machine. Thus Mani was remembered as having greatly annoyed his fellow villagers, when he was a young man, by refusing to feed himself through tilling the ground and through plucking vegetables from the lush gardens that surrounded their settlement in central Mesopotamia. Instead, he would stand outside the gardens and ask to receive his food as an act of almsgiving, as though he were a beggar.[40] For the only relation to the world of which an "elect" soul such as his own was capable was one of being as totally outside its dire processes as a beggar was outside the normal processes of the economy.

This cosmic backdrop accounts for the intensity with which the Manichaean Elect rejected the world of labor. But, as we will now see, the Manichaean Elect were not alone in their rejection of work. The grandiose and exotic cosmic myths with which Manichees justified their attitudes to the poor, to work, and to society have tended to make Manichaeism seem more exotic, more peripheral to Christianity than it was at the time. But this was by no means the case. The Manichees were radical. But they were not out of place. They came as "spiritual" Christians to enlighten their fellow Christians as to the nature of "true" Christianity. This means that the Manichees are best seen as only one—admittedly sharp—voice among many others in a vigorous debate among Christians of all kinds on *ponos*, on *'amla* (its Syriac equivalent)—on the drudgery of labor. A negative view of work as the most blatant sign of all of human bondage was central to the radical traditions of Syria as a whole—to ascetic Christians quite as much as to members of the Manichaean Elect. It is to these Syrian Christian ascetics that we must now turn.

4

"In the Likeness of the Angels": Syria and the Debate on Labor

The Background to Radicalism: The Syrian Way

In the last chapter, I showed how the radical attitude of the Manichees reflected a view of the cosmos that made the notion of alms to the poor irrelevant and the notion of work by the leaders of the Manichaean church, the Elect, repugnant. But the Manichees were not entirely exotic. They saw themselves as part of the "radical consensus" of the Christian East. Their solution was only the most drastic version, along a wide spectrum, of the notion of a spiritual exchange that reached back to the days of Saint Paul. Where they differed from contemporary Christian ascetics in Syria was in their commitment to a grandiose myth of the cosmos, to which human society was peripheral.

By contrast, the non-Manichaean holy men of Syria grappled with society in society. Their objection to work was not based on a revulsion from the material world. Rather, it reflected serious engagement with the long ache of labor in a society caught in the toils of an agrarian boom.

That an intense debate on work should have taken place in Syria is not surprising. For we must remember the presence of a very ancient past both in Syria and in Mesopotamia. These were regions that had long been preoccupied with labor. In the words of a Sumerian proverb of the third millennium BC: "*dullum* [= labor, the origin of *dal*, one of the many Hebrew words for poor] is a dog trailing behind man."[1]

This preoccupation found many forms of expression. The Akkadian *Atrahasis* myth of the second millennium BC narrated the manner in which the gods had tricked the human race into working on their behalf, while they themselves enjoyed a life of work-free relaxation.[2] The opening chapters of the book of Genesis affirmed that Adam had lost the effortless abundance of Eden and had been condemned by God to work "in the sweat of his brow" on a hard and unforgiving earth.[3] Distant echoes of these great Mesopotamian myths of the origins of labor found their way to the Aegean, and were expressed in the *Works and Days* of Hesiod. For Hesiod, the human race had been condemned to a life of perpetual toil—of *ponos*—so as to avoid "heart-rending poverty, the gift [the dubious gift] of the everlasting gods."[4] Altogether, ever since the third millennium BC, the inhabitants of Syria and Mesopotamia had attempted to explain (in the bleak words of the *Atrahasis* myth) how human beings had come "to bear the *dullum*—the drudgery—[passed on to them] by the [toilless] gods."[5]

In all these legends, work—work rendered necessary by mortality—was the curse of humankind. Seen against the background of the millennia-long history of the Fertile Crescent, the exegesis of the fall of Adam and Eve into toil that was current among radical Syrian Christians stands at the end of a long series of attempts to come to terms with labor. It was the last great effort to explain the social trauma that had resulted from the agrarian revolution of the Neolithic age, when the freedom and relative affluence of hunter-gatherer societies were replaced by the harsh discipline of the plow.[6]

So let us end by looking at the attitude to labor of a vocal section of Syrian ascetic Christianity that was contemporary with the Manichees. The theme of attitudes to work in Syrian monasticism has been brought to our attention in the past decade by two outstanding books: Philippe Escolan's *Monachisme et Église: Le monachisme syrien du ive au viie siècle*[7] and Daniel Caner's *Wandering, Begging Monks.*[8] Both books have revealed an entire third world of monastic practice, very different from our conventional view of early Christian monasticism, which is based, largely, on images of the sedentary and laborious monks of Egypt. They show that there was a "Syrian Way" to the ascetic life, which co-

TREASURE IN HEAVEN

incided neither in its practices nor in its ideology with the Egyptian model.

Indeed, it is now possible to see the Christian regions of the East as a whole (Egypt and Syria alike) as poised between two great and evenly balanced alternatives, represented by two conflicting wings of the ascetic movement. One wing was associated with the monks of Egypt. As we shall see, the monks of Egypt projected an image of ferocious self-sufficiency, in which monks neither wandered nor begged. They were expected to stay in their cells and to feed themselves by the work of their own hands. We know more about this image of monasticism because it was more fully represented in the monastic traditions of western Europe, as these had been first passed on to Latin readers by Jerome, by Augustine, and by John Cassian. It was to Egypt, not to Syria, that Benedict of Nursia looked back when he framed his famous monastic *Rule* in the early sixth century. Eventually, as a result of the diffusion of the *Rule of Saint Benedict* in the early Middle Ages, the Christian West gravitated toward the Egyptian model of the working monk.

But we have come to realize that the other wing of the ascetic movement was just as important at the time. We have to make room in our image of the early Christian world for a "Syrian way" that was quite as distinctive as was that of Egypt. The monks of Syria did not work. They claimed to have risen above labor, and to be entitled to support through the alms of the laity. They were seen as the "holy poor" par excellence. This form of monasticism tended to be treated as peripheral—if not downright suspect—in late antique and early medieval western Europe. It was not until the Franciscan movement of the thirteenth century that western Christians found that they had to grapple with an explosive combination of ascetic piety with a mendicant lifestyle. By contrast, in the Christian Middle East of the fourth and fifth centuries AD, the Syrian model was as vibrant as was the monastic model that western Europe took from Egypt. It therefore merits our close attention.

"Sons and Daughters of the Covenant": From Group Holiness to Competitive Holy Men

We must always remember, however, that there were many Syrias—just as there were many forms of sectarian Protestantism in the Burned-Over District of upstate New York in the early nineteenth century. Many of the Syrian ascetics of the time were far from being wandering beggars. Their asceticism was practiced in stolid households for the benefit of sedentary Christian communities.

Hence the importance, for scholars of early Christian monasticism, of a group known in Syriac as the *bnai* and the *bnat qiyâmâ*—the "sons and daughters of the Covenant." The institution of "sons and daughters of the Covenant" appears to have been a distinctive Syrian phenomenon. Within each church a separate category of believers emerged who had taken vows of celibacy or virginity at the moment of their baptism. This was the special "covenant" that bound them to Christ.[9] Dramatic though their vow of celibacy might be, those bound by the covenant did not abandon their local church. They remained in close contact with it. They took on the role of what sociologists would call a "primary group."[10] Their unmarried life summed up, at the very core of each Christian community, loyalty to Christ in its most incandescent form.[11]

The *bnai* and *bnat qiyâmâ* were not wanderers; still less were they beggars. They were "holy," but they were not necessarily poor. Their "holiness" consisted, rather, in their adoption of perpetual celibacy and virginity. They remained tied to their own households. Usually, they lived pious lives within the homes of their parents. What Escolan has called a tradition of "family encratism" kept them firmly rooted within the settled community.[12] Furthermore, the support of their family cushioned the financial burden to the local Christian community of such ascetic persons.

Not surprisingly, scholars have a soft spot for the "sons and daughters of the Covenant." They seem to open a window onto a very ancient Christian world. They are held to represent a distinctive, archaic form of "proto-monasticism," very different from the farouche asceticism that modern popular stereotypes have tended to associate with monks of later centuries.[13] To use the words of Francis Burkitt, who first brought them to our attention, the sons and daughters of the Covenant were "quiet, dignified and temperate."[14] They were the sort of monks that we rather wish that all monks had remained. We tend to study them as survivors from an earlier, less rigid age of Christianity, and to regret their passing as if it were the dying out of some precious species—"a remarkable ascetic tradition that went back to the very beginnings of Christianity."[15]

But this essentially backward-looking view makes it difficult for historians to understand how the sons and daughters of the Covenant could link up with more radical forms of Syrian asceticism in the course of the fourth century. In many ways the two lifestyles seemed to contradict each other. The sons and daughters of the Covenant did not enjoy the prominence of later Syrian holy men. They appear to have played a passive and somewhat faceless role in the Christian community. They were regarded as the representatives of the sanctity of a group—of the local Christian community. Scholars commonly treat them as a low-key cluster of *dévots*, little different from a well-organized church choir or a lay confraternity.[16] There seems to be no link between this quiet group and the fierce individualism that we associate with the holy men of late antique Syria such as Symeon Stylites.

Yet this view overlooks the logic of the binary relationship between holy persons and their lay admirers. Members of the Covenant did not simply form a pious backdrop to the life of each local church. They were often spoken of as "a bridge between heaven and earth."[17] They could be a seedbed that produced prominent holy men and holy women. Ephraem the Syrian (who died in 373) celebrated the baptism of one such member of the Covenant in a hymn that stressed his role as an individual mediator between God and other believers, like any other outstanding holy person:

See, the many rush at him,
With kinsmen, offspring and riches.

For whoever is baptized and puts on
The Only One, the Lord of the many,
occupies the place of [intercessor] for the many.[18]

In this situation, more radical ascetics broke free from the background of "family encratism," which tended to tie them to their local churches. I suspect that they did so in much the same way as the great wandering saints of early medieval Europe, the Irish and Anglo-Saxon *peregrini*, escaped the tribal and family monasteries that would have tied them irrevocably to their homeland. They became "strangers" by setting out to the farthest edges of northern Europe.[19] But in Syria, as we saw, holy wanderers did not have to travel very far to find some challenging "nonplace" in which to settle as riveting "strangers."

This drift away from the family and from the local community marks the beginning of what Philippe Escolan has called a *phase concurrentielle*—a phase of competitive holiness among the monks of Syria.[20] This competitive phase gathered momentum in the latter part of the fourth century and the fifth century. It reached its peak in the stunning career of Symeon Stylites (396–459). It is on this phase of competitive holy men in Syria, in the late fourth and fifth centuries, that we will concentrate. But we must never forget that such ascetic "stars" were admired because they summed up in their persons aspirations that had long existed in the Syrian tradition.

"The Labor of Angels": Work and the Fall of Adam

The work of Escolan and Caner has enabled us to recapture the distinctive features of Syrian monastic practice at this time. What I would wish to add is some consideration of the image of the human person, of society, and of nature itself that was implied in these practices. This is best approached through a consideration of Syriac traditions on the nature of the fall of Adam and Eve.

First and foremost, behind Syrian views on the Fall there lay a great sadness, which saw in the origins of labor the secret of human bondage. Like all previous narratives of the loss of a golden age when human beings had once enjoyed freedom from toil, radical Christian accounts of the fall of Adam and Eve presented human society as caught in the dull creak of labor—of *ponos*, of drudgery, of *'amla* in Syriac.

Unlike the Manichees, however, Syriac writers in the ascetic tradition did not believe that the entire material world had been corrupted. But they did believe, in no uncertain terms, that human society as a whole had fallen. Adam and Eve and their descendants had lost their first moment of sublime leisure. They had declined into the present careworn state of society. This was a society in which human beings were not only dominated by the need to work so as to eat, and thus to keep mortality at bay. They were also driven by a lust for the land that was quite as fierce as any sexual drive. This lust for the land accounted for the brutal structures of present-day society.

We have, I think, lost touch with the seriousness, even with the implied anger, of such a view of the Fall. This is because we are more used to the Augustinian tradition, in which the issue of labor was peripheral. For Augustine and his successors in the West, the fall of Adam and Eve had brought about a profound inner weakening of their individual wills. This weakening of the will was shown, in its most subtle, enduring, and (for most of us) most interesting form, in unregulated sexual desire. But this was not what was believed in the Christian East. Rather, the true fall—the fall that blotted out all others in the imagination of many Syrians—had been the fall from the work-free abundance of Eden into the present world of toil.

A vivid Syriac text of the early fifth century has recently been translated, along with a reprint of the standard edition, by Robert Kitchen and Martien Parmentier. It became known to modern scholarship under the Latin title of its first, Latin translation and commentary—the *Liber Graduum*. Its Syriac title was *Ktaba d*ᶜ*masqata: The Book of Steps*.[21] It has also been explored—and, indeed, put on the map of present-day scholarship—by an unusually thorough collection of articles that has just appeared.[22]

The *Book of Steps* enables us to relive, as it were from the inside, the dire fall into labor of Adam and Eve as this was imagined by a Syriac writer of the early fifth century. The *Book of Steps* is particularly valuable to us because of its exegesis of the fall of Adam and Eve from the garden of Eden. This exegesis did not stand on its own. It formed part of an urgent attempt to defend the notion of a Christian community structured around the ideal of a spiritual exchange between average Christians and an elite core of "Perfect" ascetics at a time (perhaps around 430) when that ideal was under pressure from critics and from proponents of rival forms of monastic organization.[23]

Not the least merit of this recent revival of interest in the *Book of Steps* is the realization that this book was not the product of an enclosed, heretical community. It was not produced by Messalian ("Praying") monks—an extremist sect whose presence (whether real or imagined) haunted many Christian authors of the late fourth and fifth centuries. It has been removed from this heresiological "pigeonhole."[24] It is also no longer seen as "the final breath of a dying form of asceticism"—as a quaint survival from an earlier stage of "proto-monasticism," and so not relevant to Syrian ascetic thought as a whole.[25] Far from it. The *Book of Steps* enables us to glimpse (if only through the eyes of a forceful and idiosyncratic preacher) many of the basic features of the spiritual landscape of radical Syria.

The author of the *Book of Steps* wrote, first and foremost, so as to urge the laity to continue to support an elite group of "angelic" Perfect Ones. For, by abandoning labor, the Perfect Ones had reversed the fall of Adam. Hence it was important for the laity to know in what way Adam had fallen, and, so, in what way the support that they offered to the Perfect Ones enabled these austere figures to bring back to their own times a touch of Paradise regained.

Throughout the *Book of Steps* laypersons were reminded that they had a clear, if subordinate, role within this binary community. They were the Upright, the Righteous Ones. They would be saved if they followed the commandments suitable to the Upright. These were the laws that God had imposed on Adam after his fall. They were straightforward moral precepts suitable to married, working persons. They included almsgiving to the poor. But the Upright were also told that one of their principal duties was to support the Perfect.[26]

To make his case, the author of the *Book of Steps* drew on a Syrian ascetic consensus as to the nature of the fall of Adam and Eve. Let us look carefully at these traditions.[27]

Adam and Eve had not known drudgery in Eden. Wrapped in contemplation, their "labor" had consisted only in the "labor of angels"—the *pôlḥana dᵉ mala'kê*.[28] This labor had not been labor on the land. Their backs had not been broken, their hands had not been hardened by "earthly" toil. Their toil, instead, had been the weightless, ethereal toil of prayer, as they joined their voices with the angels in ceaseless praise of God, their bodies swaying gently, but without violent effort, while they bowed before Him.

Through Adam and Eve's act of disobedience, the human race had fallen into many evils. It was overshadowed by death. It was exposed to the fierce ache of sexual desire. But, worst of all—because most shamefully inconsistent with Adam's first, weight-free labor of prayer as the High Priest of all creation—the human race had fallen into work: it was caught in the ancient permafrost of toil, of *'amla*.

And how had this come about? Here the author of the *Book of Steps* was careful to unravel the exact sequence of Adam's decline from Eden. The sexual element in the loss of Eden was secondary. What mattered was that Adam and Eve had rebelled against God by wishing to exercise God's power over the land. In effect, they had wished to be great landowners. They had wished to *own* the lush earth of Eden, not simply to serve God *in* Eden.

We should not overlook the raw taste of Adam's lust for the earth as this was described in the *Book of Steps*. It was no vague wandering of the mind toward material things. It was a passion that had unleashed in Adam and Eve the "demonism" of the fallen human drive toward power and possession which had continued up to the author's own days. Adam and Eve had "coveted the beauty of the earth . . . and it became an object of lust to their eyes, just as it is today."[29] Adam had both "longed for the earth" and for the power that came from possession of the earth.[30] And so the most apposite punishment for Adam consisted of having to take on the grinding toil and anxiety involved in the cultivation of the earth.[31] For this earth was no longer the abundant soil of the garden of Eden, but the hard, dry soil of the Middle East.

"In the Likeness of the Angels"

For the author of the *Book of Steps*, only the Perfect had been able to reverse the fall of Adam and Eve. They had reestablished, in the midst of a fallen humanity, a touch of the supreme leisure devoted to unceasing prayer which Adam and Eve had enjoyed in Eden. This was possible because Christ had brought back, in Himself, the "unbearable lightness" of Adam in Eden.[32] He had extended this lightness to His true followers. A few elect souls might free themselves from the world of labor, so as to devote themselves entirely to a life of prayer. These were the Perfect, the true followers of Christ. For they "have abandoned the earth . . . and attained that thing which Adam had lost."[33]

In this respect, we must remember the extent to which, in Syriac piety, Christ Himself was seen as an avatar of Adam. And so, the holy man, who followed Christ and imitated Him to the best of his ability, was an Adam in his own times. Syrian writers spoke of the holy man as a *sign*. His dramatic lifestyle was a wake-up call sent by God to challenge and to comfort a world caught in anxiety and toil.[34] This was what it meant to live the life of the *dᵉmûta dᵉ mala'kê*—life "in the likeness of the angels."[35]

But what was an angel? For the Syrians, an angel was not simply an ethereal being, hovering somewhere in the other world. An angel was a vibrant presence in this world. An angel was what an angel did. And the one thing that an angel did not do was work. Jews and Christians were agreed on this point. In the words of Rabbi Abbahu discussing the heavenly powers, "Angels are nourished by the rays of the divine presence. While with humans, if they do not labor, they may not eat."[36]

In this way, the holy men of Syria brought to their own, careworn world a touch of the life of the angels. This was a life of perpetual rapt worship. Take the example of Symeon Stylites. Symeon had installed himself on top of a tall pillar—hence his name, Symeon of the Pillar (from the Greek for pillar, *stylos*). Standing on top of his pillar, Symeon would constantly sway backward and forward with bowing motions. He did this because, so he said, he saw an angel at his side also prostrating himself in this manner before the throne of God.[37] Indeed, Symeon once did this at least 1,244 times. The thrill of this story is that we know of it because members of a bishop's retinue were standing beneath the pillar and counting every bow. They gave up at 1,244 times; but Symeon kept on bowing![38] To look at Symeon acting out the life of the angels in this fully concrete manner was to look through a society held in the grip of labor to a better world where the only toil was the enraptured worship of God.

"To Till the Hateful Earth": Land and Labor in Late Antique Syria

There was more to this current of regret for labor than mere nostalgia for the loss of a golden age. Nor should we see it only as an attempt to secure a life of constant prayer. Those who read the account of the fall of Adam and Eve (as this was interpreted by Syrian authors) or who went out to view a Stylite saint needed to know why it had become so difficult to achieve a state of leisure. Why were the demands of labor so prevalent and so over-powering? In this way, the ideal of the work-free life of "angels" was a direct challenge to modern times. The author of the *Book of Steps* had no illusions about the ills of the society in which he lived. Unlike many Christian writers, he did not believe that present-day society was bathed in the benign providence of God. For him, there was nothing providential about the division of rich and poor. Rather, in his opinion, the abrasive structures of late Roman society had been created, from the top down, by the clash of evil human wills, in defiance of the will of God. Society was what people made it; and they had made it badly. In the author's opinion, "If people did not wish it, they would not become governors and doers of evil. But because they love money and transient glory, they offer bribes and become rulers and take up the power of the sword to kill whoever they desire."[39]

Social hierarchies had no divine blessing. More remarkable still, the author of the *Book of Steps* refused to believe that God played any role in modern wars. A striking passage in the *Book of Steps* stated that, since the coming of Christ, no war can be said to have been "raised up by God." All wars were the result of human willfulness, untouched by the providence of God.[40] At best, government was "useful for this world."[41] But it was not a pretty thing. Holy persons, as imitators of the angels, looked with disabused eyes through it and through the fallen, post-Edenic society that needed such government.

But what was this society really like? Here recent research on the agrarian economy of the Middle East in late antiquity has come as a surprise to us. Through patient and wide-ranging archaeological surveys of village sites, settlement patterns, and field patterns, the stones of Syria (both in the modern state of Syria and in the wider ancient region, which includes modern Israel, Palestine, and Jordan) have come to speak to us. And they speak, loud and clear, about a triumph of hard work. In the words of Michael Decker: "Rarely, if ever, in the history of the preindustrial Mediterranean have levels of agrarian development, intensity of settlement, and a combination of security, easy communication and monetarization coalesced than they do in the late antique East."[42]

This agrarian prosperity was driven by population growth and by a sharp hunger for land. From the foothills of the Anatolian and Iranian plateaus (in eastern Turkey and northern Iraq) to the Negev (in southern Israel), cultivation pushed further afield than ever before. Behind Antioch, the mountain ridges to the east of the valleys of the Orontes and the Afrin (from the Limestone Massif in the north, through the Jebel Barisha to the Jebel al-Asa in the south) were covered with villages whose solid stone houses are still standing in a "breathtakingly good state of repair."[43] Further south, below Damascus, the volcanic landscape of the Hauran offered a similar scene. More important yet, in the fourth and fifth centuries the drive to possess the land spilled over into hitherto semidesert areas. In all these regions and beyond, the new settlers "created a striking landscape [that was the result of] a determined effort to bring Roman life, as they knew it, to the steppe."[44]

These farmers were by no means all of them great landowners. Careful study of the sizes of farm buildings, and (where these survive) of field patterns, shows that there was room in this surge of settlement for "widespread and varying wealth."[45]

Altogether, Syria has emerged from recent archaeological scholarship as the site of a late antique *Wirtschaftswunder* such as we could not have imagined had we read only the literary and theological texts of the period. Nor was this general boom of the eastern provinces restricted to the ancient heartlands of Syria. Far from it. For instance: the inhabitants of the Negev (now a largely desert area in modern southern Israel) also witnessed "one of the most successful landscape transformations in the Mediterranean in any period."[46]

The farmers of Syria represented their prosperity as a triumph of labor. Seldom, in the long history of the ancient world, have the positive results of *ponos* been flaunted with such zest. The fourth- and fifth-century Hauran produced inscriptions that praised the landowners in terms so close to the old-world values of Hesiod and of the citizen-farmers of classical Athens that only the alert eyes of Louis Robert recognized them as Christian and late Roman. One farmer was "excellent and wise in the labors of the earth"; another was "ennobled by farming."[47] The building put up in 385 by Masalemos Rabbos was built "through his very own labors as a farmer."[48] In the steppe land around Chalcis (Qennesrin), in 353, a certain Bellichos put up a granary, "out of his own toil, a beautiful work." Given the Mediterranean-wide role of large granaries as statements of the ability of the rich to hoard their grain, Bellichos's inscription celebrated his "toil" with more than usual swagger.[49]

At 'Ijaz, in inner Syria, the farmers boasted of having successfully "tilled the hateful earth."[50] This phrase, which appears on the lintel of a large farm building, was adopted by Michael Decker as the title of his remarkable book *"Tilling the Hateful*

Earth": Agricultural Production and Trade in the Late Antique East.
As Decker's book shows, the farmers of 'Ijaz who put up this inscription were feeling no pain.

The Christian church formed part of this agrarian gold rush.
In 429–30, an impressive, three-naved Church of the Apostles,
decorated with loyal inscriptions wishing victory, renewal, and
long life to the emperors, was also built in 'Ijaz.[51] These monuments to strenuous, sedentary labor were put up in exactly the
same years in which the activities of work-free monks (and the
anxieties created by their success) reached their peak.

"Devotees of Idleness": Monks and Their Critics

It is precisely this clash of perceptions that accounts in large part
for the appeal of holy men such as Symeon Stylites and of the
large groups of work-free disciples whom Symeon and many
others like him gathered around themselves. Their "angelic"
stance struck a raw nerve in the society around them. In the social imagination of their time, they had gone for the jugular. The
work-free life of these new monastic Adams challenged a central value in the world of frenetic agrarian development in which
they lived. It did this quite as effectively as did the utter poverty
of the first Franciscans, which had challenged the boom and bust
economy of the Italian cities of the high Middle Ages.

Monks were not invariably loved for doing this. Negative reactions to monks were by no means limited to pagans. Bureau-
crats and town councillors (many of them good Christians) regularly denounced the *argia*—the blatant indolence—of Christian
monks. An imperial edict issued at Beirut in 370 or 373 condemned monks as *ignaviae sectatores*, as "devotees of idleness."[52]
It is not a flattering manner for monks to make their very first
appearance in the law codes of the Roman Empire. For a contemporary pagan, such as Libanios of Antioch (314–ca. 393), the new
monks fitted all too easily into the centuries-old stereotype of the
work-shy charismatic sponger. Monks, he said, were "renegades
from the farms who claim to commune among the mountains
with the Creator of the universe."[53]

For this reason, lucubrations on the "angelic labor" of Adam (such as we have followed in the *Book of Steps*) cannot be treated as if they were part of a debate among monks alone. The debate on labor was not a storm in a teacup limited to an elite of spiritual guides, such as accounts for much monastic literature both in Christianity and in Buddhism.[54] Debates on labor were too important to be kept within the narrow circle of monks alone.

The *argia*—the idleness—of work-free monks in Syria and elsewhere was plain for all to see. The issue of whether monks should work came to be discussed all over the Mediterranean. Whenever groups of ascetics appeared or a monastery was founded, laypersons had to decide whether work-free monks were the best partners with whom to enter into a spiritual exchange. When a group of monks loyal to Syrian models arrived in Carthage around the year 400, their presence sparked off a lively debate, "so that even among laypersons, subject to a lower style of life [as nonascetics], but nonetheless fervent in their enthusiasm, rowdy disagreements began to arise."[55]

This note was made by Augustine of Hippo in 428, in the course of reviewing the book that he had written in around 403, *De opere monachorum* (*On the Work of Monks*). It gets to the nub of the matter. Augustine disapproved greatly of work-shy monks. But many laypersons positively wanted them. They wanted "angelic" figures, untarnished by labor, with whom they could enter into a vivid and satisfying form of spiritual exchange. They would seek their prayers and blessing, and would take consolation from their preaching on spiritual matters.

Hence a conflict of views which raged in a particularly explicit manner in Syria in the fourth and early fifth centuries. This is not surprising. Many members of upper-class society in Syria and throughout the Roman world still viewed the monks of their own times with the same distrust as their ancestors had viewed the outrageous religious tricksters of the second century AD. The refusal of monks to work awoke deep suspicions. This conflict of views was particularly explicit in Syria, where Greek and non-Greek, Syriac traditions—views in favor of labor and views against, expressed in either language—circulated side by side.

When dealing with this conflict, we must remember that, for members of the Greco-Roman elite, work had always been ambiguous.[56] As we have seen, for the leisured classes *ponos*—the drudgery of work—was regarded as an absolute cultural bar. It excluded those caught in toil from the supreme privileges of thought and high culture. But, in itself, *ponos* was by no means seen only as a curse and a sign of bondage, as it tended to be seen in the radical Christian tradition represented by Syriac exegesis of the fall of Adam and Eve. *Ponos* was not a total disaster. It carried positive overtones of commitment, heroic effort, and militancy that reached far beyond the labor of the fields.[57] For a landowner, even agricultural labor itself—like war, like engagement in civic affairs, like athletics—was a challenge. To use the words of William James (words chosen with superb Bostonian earnestness), such challenges "let loose in us . . . the strenuous mood."[58] Great landowners favored *ponos*—if only for others. They certainly wanted those who worked for them—the vast majority of the rural poor—to show a strenuous mood.

For a pagan such as Libanios, *ponos* was more than mere effort. It had deep religious significance. Labor in the fields was a sacred duty. It represented the human side of the bargain between the gods and humankind. Every successful harvest showed, triumphantly, the reward which the gods were prepared to bestow on those who had extracted, through hard, intelligent labor, the bounty which they, the gods, had hidden in the depths of the hard earth. To join the work-free monks in the hills was not just to shirk work. It was to "commit an injustice to the earth and to the gods."[59]

Preaching in the Greek city of Antioch, John Chrysostom thought much the same. He was as Pollyannaish on the topic of labor as was Libanios, his former teacher. John hotly contested the negative view of the fall of Adam into toil that was central to many of the ascetic traditions of Syria. "Sweat" was not imposed upon Adam as a punishment. Sweat was good for you. It was a therapy imposed on Adam by God to enable him to overcome the limitations of his fallen life on earth.[60] For Chrysostom, a

TREASURE IN HEAVEN

Christian of Greek rather than of Syrian culture, the Fall was both a comedown and an opportunity to make a fresh start.

Indeed, so upbeat was the view of work espoused by Chrysostom (and by the Greek authors—classical and Christian—on whom he drew) that later, medieval writers would derive from it an entire doctrine of technological progress. Starting with trousers ingeniously sewed together from fig leaves, humans had been challenged by the Fall to fend for themselves. They had been denied the all-too-easy abundance of Eden. But, in the long run, this was good for them. The descendants of Adam and Eve moved on briskly to the invention of the plow, to housing, to iron work, and, eventually, . . . to the building of Gothic cathedrals, decorated with carefully delineated sculptures of the labors of the months![61]

What we are dealing with is a standoff between two very different views of society in the form of a debate for and against *ponos*. It is even tempting to draw the lines of tension in this conflict across the social and geographical map of Syria. In his recent book *Economy and Society in the Age of Justinian*, Peter Sarris has argued with particular verve that we should not be misled by the solid farmhouses that fill the ridges of the Limestone Massif and elsewhere. Not all Syria was like that. Compared with the heavy grip of urban landowners on the peasantry of the rich coastal plains of the Mediterranean, from Antioch all the way down to Gaza, the hill villages of the hinterland were relatively new settlements. They still breathed the air of freedom. The hands of the great landowners had not yet come to rest upon them.[62]

It was precisely in those "marginal zones, on the edge of 'cultivation' in every sense of the word" (to use Sarris's words) that holy men such as Symeon Stylites throve.[63] They were at their most effective in landscapes that were set a little to one side of the crushing gravitational field of the great villas of the coastal plains. In the territory around Antioch, Libanios said, with palpable self-satisfaction, the rich earth "gave its gifts" with magical abundance, "without the pains of labor"—*aneu ponôn*.[64] What he omitted to say was that this abundance was the result of the unrelenting, highly disciplined labor of dependent peasants, most of whom would have been landless.[65] By contrast, the villages of the hinterland were less rigidly controlled. In the hinterland, work-free avatars of Adam were not rejected as layabouts. They were treated with awe. In a society caught in a frenzy of labor, they had opened a window onto another, more ancient, and more free world.

"To Reap the Blessing of That Holy Hand": Monks and Their Lay Supporters

In this respect, it is worthwhile noting that the hagiography of the Syrian world shows a remarkable degree of involvement on the part of holy men in the resolution of social grievances. In his vivid *History of the Monks of Syria*, Theodoret of Cyrrhus recounted the manner in which a holy village priest had cursed the cart onto which a well-known Antiochene landowner had loaded more than his fair share of the peasants' harvest.[66] Symeon Stylites was known to have regulated rates of interest for entire villages.[67] Alexander the Sleepless[68] and, later, the holy man Habib of Amida (Diyarbakır, modern Turkey) ranged the banks of the Euphrates, challenging landowners to burn their collections of debtors' bonds—the most pervasive instrument of all for the enslavement of the peasantry.[69] Persons such as the author of the *Book of Steps* had no doubt that they were looking out over a fallen world. They lived in the shadow of Adam's first, tragic "longing" for the earth. In the words of Ephraem the Syrian, in the late fourth century, only the sweat of Christ that fell from the Cross could redeem an earth soaked, for millennia, in the sweat of Adam's brow.[70]

Altogether, the exegesis of the fall of Adam and Eve, combined with many dramatic incidents in the lives of the saints of Syria, tempts us to view this literature as a literature of protest, even as a manifestation of the "religion of the oppressed." But what this view overlooks is the remarkable capacity of Syrian Christianity to use the notion of the spiritual exchange to bring together persons of widely differing classes, differing levels of culture, and differing languages around the figures of holy men.

We need only turn to the most urbane work of hagiography of the time, the *History of the Monks of Syria*, written by Theodoret of Cyrrhus in 440, to realize the tenacity and the density of the filaments of spiritual exchange that reached out from the Syrian hinterland to touch the heart of privileged families in Antioch. Each family or group of friends had their own holy man to whom they turned in order "to reap the blessing of that holy hand," in the form of teaching, healing, intercessory prayer, and arbitration.[71]

Theodoret's accounts of the holy men around Antioch amount, at times, to a family history. His mother had been cured of infertility and helped through the dangers of a near lethal pregnancy by the prayers of one holy man, Peter.[72] On one occasion Peter cut his belt in two: "He put one half of it around his own waist and the other half round mine. My mother often put it on me when I was ill, and often on my father. . . . Many of her acquaintance who had discovered this constantly took the girdle to help the sick."[73] As a child, little Theodoret went out regularly to the mountain above Antioch to meet Peter and his companion, Daniel. Old Daniel "often set me on his knees and fed me with grapes and bread."[74]

But these apparently weight-free ascetic idylls were based on a constant, discreet flow of material goods. We only learn in passing that the famous holy man Macedonius, named "The Barley Eater" for his preference for coarse gruel (as near as possible to raw, uncooked food) over manufactured bread, received his supply of barley from the family of Theodoret.[75] One should add that this could amount to a lot of barley. Holy men were credited with miraculously small appetites. But, as Philippe Escolan points out, holy men were seldom alone. They were surrounded by virtual monasteries of disciples, many of whom had been recruited from persons they had healed or otherwise helped. By the time of Theodoret, each one of these monasteries could shelter as many as 150 to 400 monks. All of these had to be fed, housed, and clothed.[76] Work-free holy men, though they may have appeared as beings as free as the birds, were not cheap.

But, whatever the complexity of the situation on the ground (which included the ease with which holy men could succumb to the patronage of rich donors), these angelic holy persons, by abandoning work, had established a model of the ascetic life that challenged contemporaries to think again about the building blocks of their own society. And they had done so in the midst of one of the most hard-worked and successful regions in the late Roman Middle East.

It is against the background of the debates on labor which took place in Syria in the fourth and fifth centuries that we should place the very different answer presented by the monks of Egypt. By taking a stance on the issue of labor—by insisting that a monk should work—the monks of Egypt deliberately rejected a central feature of the form of the ascetic life which had flourished in Syria and which threatened, also (in its most extreme form, through Manichaean missionaries), to make its way far up the valley of the Nile. And so, it is to Egypt, as the great alternative to the religious ebullience of the Fertile Crescent, that we will turn in the next two chapters.

5

"The Work of the Hands . . . an Ornament to the Men of Egypt": Monks and Work in Fourth-Century Egypt

"A People Made Better by Blessed Poverty": Monks and Money

Pagans who witnessed the rise of Christian monasticism in the fourth century AD did so with notably disabused eyes. What shocked them about the ascetic movement were not necessarily, or exclusively, the features that tend to shock modern persons—the otherworldliness, the self-mortification that seemed to border on masochism, the denial of sex. Instead, what struck them most forcibly was the link between monks and money. For them, monks were no more than peculiarly shameless avatars of the charismatic panhandlers and tricksters whom we met, in our second chapter, in the second century AD. The fact that monks were work shy proved that they were successful scroungers. They lived a life of indolence from the wealth of others. Writing against his contemporary the Cynic philosopher Heracleius, the emperor Julian wrote, in AD 362:

> Long ago I gave you a nickname. . . . It is "renouncers" [*apotak-tistai*], a name applied to certain persons by the impious Gali-laeans. They are for the most part men who by making small sacrifices gain much or rather everything from all sources. . . . Something like that is your method, except perhaps that they [the monks] utter divine revelations [as the Cynics do not] and [unlike the Cynics] they levy tribute on specious pretexts . . . which they call "alms."[1]

We already meet the term *apotaktikos*—renouncer—as the equivalent for monk in Egyptian papyri of the 340s.[2] But Julian himself may have heard the term used when he was in exile in Cappadocia. For it was also applied to the celibate leaders of sectarian groups in the hinterland of Asia Minor.³ A century later, by the end of the fifth century AD, the monks appeared, to disgruntled pagans, to be everywhere and to have come to own everything. In the words of Count Zosimus, the author of the *New History*, writing in Constantinople in around AD 500: "From that time to this, they have taken over most of the land and, under the pretext of giving everything to the poor, have reduced almost everyone else to beggary."⁴

We have traced the long-term roots of the situation observed by hostile pagans. Whether they were Manichees or Christians, many ascetics claimed that they were the "holy poor." They were the "little ones," the true disciples of Christ. Those who gave to them were certain to receive a heavenly reward: *"And whosoever gives to one of these little ones even a cup of cold water, because he is a disciple . . . he shall receive his reward"* (Matt. 10:42). This citation was widely used, for instance, by the Manichaean Elect in favor of almsgiving to themselves.⁵

For such persons, to be a member of the "holy poor" did not in any way mean that one experienced the helplessness of the real, working poor. Far from it. It meant the ability to rise entirely above work through the support of others. Poverty meant freedom from care. An original letter of Mani has been discovered at Kellis and only recently published. In it, Mani spoke of his Elect as a "people made better by Blessed Poverty."⁶ "Blessed Poverty" was as real to the Manichaean Elect (as also to the "angelic" holy men of Syria) as was Lady Poverty to Saint Francis. And, as with the Franciscans and the other mendicant orders of high medieval Europe, the issue was who would foot the bill and on what terms. How could a group of persons live from the labor of others, in a permanent state of miraculous lightness of being, without being dismissed (as pagans dismissed them) as mere parasites?

Unlike the Manichees, the holy men of Syria did not exclude the poor from their field of vision. Perched on top of his pillar, committed to prayer alone and supported by the offerings of his disciples and of the faithful, Symeon Stylites never claimed that

TREASURE IN HEAVEN

he was the only poor person entitled to receive alms. Indeed, he was believed to have debated the issue with none other than the prophet Elijah, who appeared to him in a vision: "He pondered and reflected about who really are the poor. The crippled and poor who beg? Or the oppressed? Or those of whom the blessed Apostle [Paul] speaks, *the holy ones* [Rom. 15:25] who live in the mountains [the monks and hermits]?" The prophet reassured him: "You should be equally concerned about all mankind: the crippled, the poor who beg, your brother monks. . . . You should also be concerned about God's priests."[7]

But there was no doubt that, in most of Syria, persons such as Symeon (whether established on pillars or not) were regarded as privileged. As Symeon's near contemporary, the author of the *Book of Steps*, made plain, the care of the local poor could be delegated to a solid infrastructure of married and hard-working Christians—the Upright. But the Upright were also obliged to support the Perfect Ones—great ascetics such as Symeon, who brought into the careworn world of Syria a touch of the prayerful leisure of Adam.

"The Work of the Hands . . . an Ornament to the Men of Egypt": The Creation of an Image

Dramatic though these forms of mendicant asceticism might have been, as they spread throughout the Syriac-speaking world in the late third, fourth, and early fifth centuries AD, they were met by an alternative constellation of expectations, primarily (though never exclusively) associated with Egypt. In Egypt, monks did not live from alms. They worked to support themselves.

So it is to Egypt that we must now turn. In this chapter we will pay particular attention to the manner in which an "authorized" representation of the "true" monk—the monk as he should be— was constructed. This happened within two generations. We begin with a book that quickly became a classic: the *Life of Anthony*, written by the patriarch Athanasius in AD 357. We end with another classic—the *Lausiac History* of Bishop Palladius. This was a description, almost a gazetteer, of the monks of Egypt and elsewhere. It was presented to Lausus, a high-placed eunuch in the imperial court at Constantinople, in AD 420 (hence its title: *The History Presented to Lausus*).

Seldom has the image of the protagonists of a nascent movement been put together so rapidly and with such lasting effect as was the authorized image of the monks of Egypt as universally committed to work. Yet this image has been shown by modern scholars to have largely been based on a drastic simplification of reality. If this was so, we still have to ask why it was simplified, and simplified in this particular direction. The historian has to ask what wider considerations, at this precise time—the late fourth and early fifth centuries—gave credence and resonance to the image of the Egyptian monk as a man of labor rather than as a work-free "angel," in the manner of the monks of Syria. These two chapters will attempt to do this.

But first let us set the scene. Egypt lay at the extreme southwestern end of the Fertile Crescent. It was far from being a world locked into itself. From the end of the third century onward, the entire length of the Nile valley was more open to the social and religious ferment of the Mediterranean and the Fertile Crescent than at any other period in its long history. Indeed, the most significant advance in the modern study of late antique Egypt has been the realization of the extent to which the valley of the Nile cannot be treated in splendid isolation from the rest of the late Roman world. A series of vivid monographs, from Roger Bagnall's *Egypt in Late Antiquity* (of 1993) to the recent study of Ariel López, *Shenoute of Atripe and the Uses of Poverty*, have made plain the manner in which, in the words of López, "As the empire's center of gravity moved towards the east and therefore much closer, Egypt was drawn fully and inexorably into late Roman civilization."[8]

We have already seen this in the case of the Manichaean missionaries. Within a few generations, they had made their way far up the valley of the Nile, leaving precious deposits of documents in the Fayyum and in the distant Dakhlah oasis. "Syrian" forms of asceticism were also present. A recently published papyrus reveals a Stylite hermit established outside Antinoë/Antinoöpolis

(Sheikh 'Ibada) in the Thebaid. It is a rental agreement by which the Stylite arranges for a donkey to bring a regular supply of water to the monastery that has, apparently, grown up at the foot of his column. Even if, in this case, "Stylite" may have been no more than an honorific title for a prominent monk, the papyrus showed that a markedly Syrian form of asceticism could be at home in Egypt.[9]

Altogether, it was quite possible for a monk in the valley of the Nile to carry "a Syria in the Mind," and to feel drawn to forms of the "angelic" lifestyle represented by the monks of Syria. No insuperable cultural, social, or ecological barrier blocked the open road from the Fertile Crescent into Egypt. What came to stand in the way of such an option was a representation of the lifestyle of the "true" monk that was constructed with great care so as to place work and not freedom from work at the very center of the image of the monks of Egypt. To put it briefly: Egyptian monks did not have to be men of labor. It was a choice on their part. And, as we shall see, it was a choice with profound implications for the relations between Egyptian society and the ascetic movement, and—deeper yet—for the image of humanity that was condensed in this choice.

In order to understand the development of the Egyptian image of the monk, we must begin with the well-known figure of Saint Anthony. It was in the Fayyum in around AD 270—that is, less than a decade before the death of Mani in AD 277 and well over a generation before the conversion of Constantine in AD 312—that a young man called Anthony decided to move out from his village. He was a comfortable farmer. As the owner of an estate of some two hundred acres, he would have been among the largest landowners in the region. It was said that he had been converted by hearing in a church the crucial passage from the Gospel of Matthew with which we began this book: "Just then it happened that the Gospel was being read, and he heard the Lord saying to the Rich Young Man: *'If you would be perfect, go, sell what you possess and give to the poor, and you will have treasure in heaven'*" (Matt. 19:21).[10]

Though hailed in all later ages as the Father of all Hermits—

as the originator of Christian desert monasticism—Anthony did not start from scratch. He grew up in a world where varied forms of Christian asceticism were already clearly visible. He was faced by many choices. For this reason, it is important to note that, at the time of his renunciation, Anthony was presented as having chosen to take steps that were significantly different from the pattern established by his contemporaries, the vibrant holy men of Syria and the missionaries of the "Holy Church" of Mani. Anthony did not take to the roads. He took to the desert and stayed there. Even if, for the first part of his life as an ascetic, this desert was within walking distance of the settled land,[11] Anthony stayed clear of the network of roads and river transport that had enabled the Manichaean missionaries to move with such ease.

Furthermore, Anthony's renunciation was accompanied by a dramatic act of almsgiving to the "real" poor: "Selling all the rest of his portable wealth [his house, furniture, silverware, and clothes], when he had collected all the cash realized by this sale, he gave it to the poor."[12]

Last but not least, once he had divested himself of his wealth, Anthony refused to receive alms for himself. Although established in the desert, Anthony was believed to have maintained himself throughout his life by the work of his own hands. From then onward, the words ascribed to Paul in the Second Letter to the Thessalonians (words that, whether they were originally his own or not—a modern doubt that late antique Christians did not raise—showed Paul at his most anxious to avoid the accusation of being a charismatic freeloader) became the mantra of the monks of Egypt: *"For even when we were with you, we gave you this command: If any one will not work, let him not eat"* (2 Thess. 3:10).[13]

Or so the story goes. We should remember that the only account of the conversion of Anthony that has come down to us was written eighty years after the event. It is the *Life of Anthony*, written immediately after his death in 356, by none other than Athanasius, the great bishop of Alexandria. It was written at a time when Athanasius, faced by the determination of the court to oust him as a troublemaker from the see of Alexandria, had fallen back on the religious networks of the Nile valley. The *Life of Anthony* sealed the alliance between Athanasius and the newly emergent monks of Egypt that had already developed over decades. But the *Life* was not written for internal consumption. It was written very much "for export." It was addressed to foreign monks, and was sent out in haste (so Athanasius claimed) before the winter season closed the seas.

The *Life of Anthony* was written to tell these overseas monks, in no uncertain terms, what a monk should be like. It is usually assumed that the persons interested in the monks of Egypt were westerners, from Rome and Gaul. But the coasts of Syria and Asia Minor also lay on a busy sea route that led from Alexandria to Constantinople. Those who read the *Life of Anthony* in those regions may have been better aware than were the distant westerners of the alternative presented by the "angelic" monasticism of Syria, whose coasts were passed every year by the grain fleets that sailed from Alexandria to Constantinople.

Faced by this extensive audience of westerners and of inhabitants of the eastern Mediterranean, Athanasius presented Anthony very much as a "literary icon"—to use the well-chosen term of James Goehring.[14] It was a "literary icon" painted with great care. The story of Anthony was Athanasius's considered answer to patterns of ascetic behavior of which he did not approve.[15]

Indeed, behind the crisp lines of the *Life of Anthony*, we can catch the hint of a debate between Syria and Egypt which had already rumbled for over half a century. In Egypt, the act of renunciation itself and the subsequent relations between monks and the society around them were presented, as in the *Life of Anthony* (and in all subsequent Egyptian sources—and especially in those written for outside consumption), in tacit contrast to forms of ascetic behavior that were taken for granted in Syria and in other parts of the Fertile Crescent.

Athanasius's portrait of Anthony is, indeed, very like an icon. The bright colors (as hard and bright as the encaustic paint of a Fayyum mummy portrait) created a magical "reality effect." They still hold our gaze today. But it is only by looking at the ascetic world in the Middle East as a whole, in Syria as well as in Egypt, that we realize that this portrait had been painted from a palette of colors that denied at every point an alternative icon, based on a different color scheme. The *Life of Anthony* proves (on closer inspection) to have been based on the denial of an ever-present, unspoken alternative. Egypt was not—and would never be—Syria.

As we know, Athanasius's portrait of Anthony became canonical in most of Egypt and, eventually, in large parts of the Christian world. In particular, his distinctive view of Anthony determined the image of Egyptian monasticism which visitors from foreign lands took back with them to their home regions—to Gaul, to Italy, to Constantinople and Anatolia.

Nothing shows this more clearly than does a phrase that exists only in the Coptic version of the famous *Lausiac History* of Palladius. Palladius first visited Egypt between AD 388 and 400. But he did not present the final version of his *History* until AD 420. It appears that Palladius had written earlier drafts of this *History*. One of these drafts has survived in a Coptic translation. This is an exciting discovery. It means that we can catch an echo of the first impressions of a foreign visitor to Egypt in the late 380s—no more than a generation after Athanasius's *Life of Anthony*. The message that Palladius had picked up in Egypt was clear. Egyptians were both men of the desert *and* men of work: "For that, indeed, is their great glory, *as is also* [Palladius was careful to add] the work of the hands which is an ornament to the men of Egypt."[16]

What is remarkable is the speed with which the Egyptian image of the working monk was brought into play in a widespread debate on work that had been provoked by Syrian practices. This debate swept around the Mediterranean like a tidal wave. In 374, Epiphanius of Salamis appealed to the example of the monasteries of Egypt in his refutation of the work-shy, "praying monks"—the Messalians—of Mesopotamia. These Syrians needed to learn to work: "As is the case in every monastery of Egypt and in other regions they are at work . . . like bees building up a honeycomb."[17]

In 384, Jerome painted an equally emphatic picture of the disciplined workload of the Pachomian monasteries of Upper

Egypt. He did this for the benefit of upper-class Roman read-ers.[18] In 388, Augustine (at that time a recent convert from Man-ichaeism) did the same. He compared the idle and vagrant life-style of the Manichaean Elect with that of the monks of Egypt. He himself had come to know of Egyptian-style monasteries in Milan and Rome. In them, the monks "were not in any way a burden to others, but lived in the manner of the East [*Orientis more*], and followed the authority of the Apostle Paul by spend-ing their time at work with their hands."[19]

In his description of the monasteries of Egypt, Augustine added the telling detail that the monks not only supported them-selves. Their industrious handicrafts also enabled them to pile up surpluses. These surpluses were instantly shipped down the Nile to clothe and feed the poor in distant cities.[20] By around 396, the Latin version of the *Historia Monachorum in Aegypto*, prepared by Rufinus of Aquileia, repeated this claim.[21]

In 403, Augustine returned to the theme. As we saw in our last chapter, he had been prompted by fierce debates among the laity concerning a group of work-less monks in the Syrian style who had appeared in Carthage. In the *De opere monachorum, On the Work of Monks*, Augustine was definite. Monks were obliged to work. They had to work because Saint Paul had worked. With characteristic thoroughness, Augustine tried to explain exactly how Paul had worked. Given the frenetic religious activities of the Apostle, this was not an altogether easy thing to do: "if the Apostle did physical work . . . what was that work and when did he find the time both to work and to preach the Gospel? I simply do not know . . . who can calculate his work habits, the way he distributed his time?"[22]

It is a revealing admission. The image of Paul as a worker was essential to the self-image of the monks of Egypt. In this, they followed a wider development. The last decades of the fourth century have been called the "generation of S. Paul."[23] This was not only because of the theological problems that Paul's letters had raised. In the Greek East, particularly, Paul emerged ever more sharply as a biographical subject. He was seen not only as a source of dogma but as a person with a distinctive life that many wished to imagine in detail so as to imitate it in their own times. As Michael Williams has made plain in an excellent recent study, *Authorized Lives*, the interest in Paul as a model for the behavior of every monk reflected the warm optimism of a section of the monastic movement. Many believed that the golden days of the early church had returned to Egypt. Monks who left the "world" found themselves in a time warp. They could think of themselves as "inhabiting a permanent Biblical present."[24]

The figure of the Apostle Paul was very much part of this "permanent Biblical present." Paul provided a cogent model of monastic behavior. The "manner of the East" was, in effect, the "manner of Saint Paul." It is this which accounts for the rapid emergence of the image of Paul as a monastic Stakhanovite. For Paul was determined to be dependent on no one. This was Paul as he was presented in 2 Thessalonians 3:8: *"We did not eat any-one's bread without paying, but with toil and labor we worked day and night, that we might not burden any of you."*

By the fifth century, the image of the working monk, based on the image of Saint Paul, was fully in place. Consulted by the bishops of Antinoë/Antinoöpolis (Sheikh 'Ibada) about monks who claimed to pray but not to work, the answer of the great abbot Shenoute of Atripe (385–466) was firm: "The holy apostle, he was yesterday, he is today and forever when he says, *Whoever does not want to work, let him not eat* [2 Thess. 3:10]. That is wisdom truly perfect."[25] Shenoute, we should note, was an exact contemporary of Symeon Stylites. In the self-image of the monks of Egypt, the door to Syria was well and truly slammed shut.

Nothing shows this more clearly than do the *Apophthegmata Patrum*, the *Sayings of the Desert Fathers*. This remarkable collection of the sayings of leading monks in Egypt was put together in the middle or even toward the end of the fifth century. The collection was not made in Egypt itself. It was put together by Egyptian monks living in Palestine. Palestine lay on the border between the two different worlds of monastic piety. Many of the anecdotes and sayings preserved in the *Apophthegmata Patrum* were shots across that border. They were challenges to the "angelic" holy men of Syria. They implied that a silent war had been waged between the monastic traditions of Syria and Egypt, and that the wisdom of Egypt had prevailed. There was no room, in Egypt at least, for "angelic" wannabes:

> It was said of John the Dwarf, that one day he said to his elder brother, "I would like to be free of all care, like the angels, who do not work, but ceaselessly offer worship to God." So he took off his cloak and went away into the desert. After a week he came back to his brother. When he knocked on the door, he heard his brother say . . . "Who are you?" He said, "I am John, your brother." But he replied, "But John has become an angel, and henceforth he is no longer among men." . . . His brother did not let him in, but left him there in distress until morning. Then, opening the door, he said to him: "You are a human being and you must work again in order to eat." Then John made a prostration before him and said, "Forgive me."[26]

Image and Reality in Late Roman Egypt: Modern Approaches

The widespread crystallization of a classic image of the monks of Egypt ensured that the realities of Egyptian monasticism, "on the ground" as it were, quietly sank from view. They were pushed to one side by a pervasive need to present the monks in terms of a highly stylized representation that canceled out, at every point, rival images of the true monk that were prevalent in other Christian regions.

It does not come as a surprise, therefore, that those who study the monastic movement in Egypt tend to be divided into two camps. On the one hand, those who study the evidence of the papyri and of the monastic archaeology of Egypt are acutely aware of the hiatus between monastic self-presentation in written texts and the realities of monastic life. In the severe words of Roger Bagnall: "Here, if ever, [when faced by such texts] 'hermeneutical suspicion' will be warranted."[27]

Some of the very best studies of late Roman Egypt and of the place of monasticism in Egyptian society have come from this critical tradition. For such scholars, ideologically motivated sources like Athanasius's *Life of Anthony* and Palladius's *Lausiac History* are fair game. Papyrologists pride themselves—and often with good reason—on being able to demystify the monks. They stress the difference between "an ideal picture, *réalité narrative,* and . . . *réalité vécue*"—the real, day-to-day life of Egyptian monasticism.[28] For such scholars, the canonical sources for the monastic movement offer only misleading stereotypes. These stereotypes are of little use "if one wishes to understand Egyptian monasticism as it was in the real world."[29] In the blunt words of Ewa Wipszycka, the doyenne of the study of the social and economic role of the Christian church in Egypt: "Patrologists and historians of monasticism know nothing about ancient economy."[30]

Furthermore, a lively tradition of literary criticism has come to be applied to the study of early Christian texts. In this tradition—to use the words of Susannah Elm—it is "the author who emerges as full blooded."[31] What holds the attention of scholars are the literary devices by which authors of the classics of early Egyptian monasticism constructed their image of the monks of Egypt. This literary play ensured that the idea of the Egyptian desert and of its industrious monastic inhabitants arrived "packaged and fetishized"[32] on the shores of western Europe and elsewhere. Whether these literary texts referred in any way to a reality "on the ground," or were simply reflections of the talents of their authors—and, one must add, of the literary acumen of those who now interpret them—is treated as being of secondary importance.

These two developments have effectively overshadowed the study of the monks of Egypt. It seems as if "text" and "reality" have drifted further apart than ever before. It is time to attempt to bring the two traditions a little closer together. I would like to ask, inevitably very briefly, what it was in the context of Egypt itself that accounted for the weight of this particular image among the monks of Egypt. What immediate problems did it address? Above all, what was the imaginative logic that accounted for its tenacity in the Egypt of the fourth and fifth centuries? But first we must look more closely at the image of the laborious monk itself.

The Laborious Monk

For those of us who emerge from a reading of the major Egyptian monastic texts of the fourth and early fifth centuries, the most lasting impression of the image of the monk in Egypt which these texts convey is not that the image is wildly exaggerated, nor even that it is suspiciously repetitive (that it is a mere array of topoi), but that it is highly abstracted. Monks (and nuns—but it is mainly monks who will concern us here) are reduced to their bare essences. Their lives are compressed right down into a few clear strokes. They are matchstick figures, more often defined by what they are not than by what they are.

First and foremost, monks were presented as "thingless" persons. *Aktémosyné*—the studied absence of possessions—is used more often to describe their state than is the word "poverty." We are told that laypersons who entered monasteries (such as that of Pachomius) were struck by the utter dispossession of the monks in matters of food and clothing.[33] To upholders of true thinglessness, even a row of books lying in an alcove was an unwelcome sight.[34] Stripped down to bare essentials in this way, monks were presented as being nothing but their bodies. Social nudists, they were thought of as facing hunger and sexual desire with an immediacy that lent an air of gripping physicality to all monastic literature.[35]

Reduced to their bodies, monks were presented as having to preserve that body through taking in food and through shielding it with clothing. What for Paul (or his disciples, the possible authors of the Letters to Timothy) had been a gnomic platitude— *but if we have food and clothing with these let us be content* (1 Tim. 6:8)—carried a heavy charge in Egyptian monastic literature: these two basic human needs glowed like an incandescent wire in all accounts.

For "thingless" persons, neither food nor clothing could be

taken for granted. The only way to these necessities was work. Hence the hands of these matchstick figures were presented as being in constant motion. Daily needs had to be met by daily work.

As this work was presented, it was, in many ways, peculiar work. It was nonwork. It was work abstracted from the normal rhythms of agrarian life. Monks could work at their little gardens. But it was far less certain that they should work, like peasants, to draw sustenance from the lush fields.[36] In reality, monks often took part in the great annual spasm of the harvest. But they were presented as doing so on the same footing as landless laborers and other social casualties (impoverished men and women) who, for a short, burning season, filled the fields of the landowners with frenetically busy hands.[37]

Harvest labor by monks was mentioned in monastic texts so as to drive home the message of "thinglessness" with especial force. Nothing of those rich fields would be theirs unless the owner of the field (like God) agreed to give them a tiny share of the cut grain and the fallen ears.[38] The monks were as outside wealth—wealth as defined by the possession of land—as were the poorest gleaners "among the alien corn."[39]

Rather, the work that was privileged in monastic accounts was thought of as work that continued day in and day out in a manner that contrasted sharply with "real" work. Real work was tied to the changing seasons and to the great rising and ebbing of the Nile. But the work of monks was timeless work. It consisted of basketwork and of other kinds of plaiting. Monks were presented as producing baskets ("the 'plastic' bags of antiquity"),[40] sieves, fans, ropes. Not all of this was light, token work. Large monasteries with sufficient manpower produced heavy hawsers, woven from alfalfa grass, for the great boats of the Nile.[41] Such work drew on raw materials that came from the margins of society—straw, reeds, the fronds of date palms. Even if these materials were more available at some seasons than at others, they nonetheless enabled the monks to produce plaited goods throughout the year.

Such work was presented as being eminently apposite work for men reduced to their bare essentials: "They said of Abba

Megethius, that. . . . He owned nothing in this world, except a knife with which he cut reeds and every day he made three small baskets, which was all he needed for his food."[42]

Needless to say, a considerable element of abstraction went into this particular image of the relations of monks with the economy and ecology of normal society. But the image ensured that the work of the monks was seen as, above all, work set free from time. It was thought of as being above the seasons and even above the alternation of night and day. Relatively light, sheltered, and potentially unending, the image of the monk at work that was projected in monastic circles was considerably more like the work of women than it was like the heavy, spasmodic labor of male peasants.[43]

This work was presented as unending because it was held to guarantee (and, indeed, to certify) the unending independence of the monk. When the good monk lay dying, he was expected to remember his life as a life of independence maintained by work. On his deathbed, the great Apa Pambo swore, "From the time when I came into the desert here and built my cell and dwelt here, I do not recall having eaten *bread for nothing* [*dôrean arton*, "bread as a gift," 2 Thess. 3:8], but only that which was the work of my own hands."[44]

The end product of all this work had to be sold so as to raise money for food and clothing. No matter how much monks might wish to be independent of the wider world, the very means by which they gained their independence brought them into contact with it. The engagement of monks in the real economy of Egypt should not be seen as an inconsistency or a sign of weakness. It was a highly charged paradox. Contacts between monks and the local market were presented as being fraught with danger. They were constantly patrolled and cut down to a minimum. They were endlessly talked about. It was as if the link to the market-place was maintained almost on purpose. It acted as a perpetual, charged reminder of the nagging link that bound the body to the soul, and the monk to his fellow humans.[45]

Last but not least—and most surprising of all—this work was never presented as if it was directed toward subsistence alone. It was work for a surplus. It brought into dramatically sharp focus the ancient Christian demand that the surplus (the *to perisseuma* of Paul's letters: 2 Cor. 8:14) of a Christian community—and by extension of each Christian household—should be given in whole or in part to the poor. Monks in Egypt were expected to create that surplus and to give it all to the poor. Briefly, they were to act as ideal Christian householders.

In the case of the monks, the flow of wealth from subsistence to surplus, and from surplus to the poor, was presented with merciless precision. Economic historians of the later Roman Empire depend on monastic anecdotes for much of what they know about wages and the cost of living among the working poor. For these monastic anecdotes are filled with statistics. The monk measured, with anxious (or proud) precision, the exact sums that he received for his work, the sums that he spent on his food, and the sums that he gave, as surplus, as alms to the poor.[46]

So much for the ideal portrait of the monk. It goes almost without saying that real life was not like this. Papyrus evidence from the fourth century shows that monks often owned property.[47] Despite the insistence of later theorists of monasticism, such as John Cassian (who wrote in the 420s in distant Marseilles), monks were not expected to divest themselves of private wealth in favor of their monastery. This did not happen until the age of Justinian.[48] As Ewa Wipszycka remarked, with her habitual good sense: in the fourth century, converts to the ascetic life had to face quite enough privations on becoming *apotaktikoi*—renouncers—without adding to these the complexities and dangers involved in cutting themselves off entirely from their family property.[49]

Nor did the monks invariably inhabit aseptically empty cells. The excavations of the late fifth-century hermitages of Esna, in Upper Egypt, show that those who faced the privations of the desert often did so only an hour's walk away from the settled land. They occupied carefully constructed buildings, with shaded courtyards and vents to circulate cool air. In the words of Roger Bagnall, they "clearly lived lives of self-mortification in a setting designed to remind them of wealth not poverty."[50]

TREASURE IN HEAVEN

Altogether, in the relation of the monks to property, to housing, and to culture, the monastic movement of fourth-century Egypt had a strong element of what the modern French call *bobo*—the bourgeois bohemian. Many monks were landed gentry. Many have been revealed, by modern scholars, to have been fully paid up intellectuals in the teaching tradition of the great Origen. (Indeed, such are the pendulum swings in modern scholarship that, only a generation ago, we thought that Athanasius and other Greek authors were guilty of having dressed up Egypt's rude sons of the soil as classical philosophers. Now it is the other way round: even Anthony has been presented as an intellectual masquerading as a peasant!)[51]

To have discovered the extent of this upper-class element in the intellectual and social life of the early monks is one of the great achievements of modern scholarship. We now know that we are dealing with a movement whose protagonists drew on many different traditions and reflected the horizons of many different layers of Egyptian society.[52]

This diversity played a crucial role in the emergence of the authorized image of the monk. In so mixed a movement, it was crucial to reach some consensus as to exactly what were the parameters of the monastic life. What made a "true" monk in Egypt? The creation of an ideal image of the monk was not a mere ideologically driven deformation. Nor was it an entirely rhetorical construct. The image of the monk played an active role in the creation of consensus within a socially and culturally diverse movement. Those who wanted to be monks had to know what a monk was. They needed an image to steer toward. We should not be unduly surprised or unnecessarily suspicious if this image emerged as highly stylized.

Indeed, if great social and cultural diversity had not characterized the monastic movement in Egypt, monastic literature would never have been as abundant or as vivid as it was. Like the literatures of other great ascetic movements—one thinks of the immense Vinaya literature of Buddhist northern India so ably exploited by Gregory Schopen[53]—much of the monastic literature of Egypt was addressed by monks to fellow monks. It showed monks engaged in hot disputes among themselves as to what were the true forms of monasticism.

For this reason, the vignettes that hold our attention cannot be treated as straightforward snapshots of the monastic life of Egypt. But nor can they be dismissed as mere cover-ups or willful distortions of reality. At the time, they were advanced in support of vigorous arguments with opponents who were often fellow monks, and especially with monks from other regions (whether real or imagined) who upheld differing approaches to the common ascetic enterprise.

The very abstractness of these vignettes—their matchstick-man quality—enabled them to function, as it were, as "Ideal Types." They were patterns to which monks at all levels might refer their actions. We should not underestimate the long-term power of these vignettes. In a refreshingly alert study of the relation between literature and reality in late antiquity, Peter Turner has pointed out that the dichotomy between text and reality was often blurred. Seemingly stereotypical narratives and images became internalized. They came to act, as it were, as unspoken guidelines, fostering one course of action and inhibiting another. As a result, there was "a much greater continuity between written texts and the lives they relate than is usually accepted."[54]

Hence the interest for us of the images of the monk that we meet most frequently in fourth- and fifth-century texts—from Athanasius's *Life of Anthony* to the *Sayings of the Desert Fathers.* They are precious to us not only for what they tell us or do not tell us about the real monasticism of Egypt. They also enable us to listen to a debate by which the ascetic movement of a major Christian region (in this case, Egypt) talked itself into a distinctive form, significantly different from that of its Middle Eastern neighbors. And this difference lay (in the words of John Cassian) in an attitude to work. It was the Egyptians "who share a special concern about work"—*quibus maxime cura est operis.*[55] Work was what made them special. In our next chapter, let us see why this was the case.

6

"You Are a Human Being . . . You Must Work . . . in Order to Eat": The Meanings of Work in Monastic Egypt

"In Spirit I Have Come to Your Feet": Monks and Their Lay Patrons

In our last chapter, we made plain the extent to which the classic image of the monks of Egypt was the fruit of a conscious choice. It charged with particular significance the fact that the monks of Egypt worked for their living. The denial of an alternative view of the monk—as a work-free "angel," such as had been current in Syria—formed an all-pervasive background to these texts. The hiatus between the image of the laboring monk in monastic literature and the down-to-earth realities revealed by papyrology and by monastic archaeology in Egypt only serves to heighten the distinctiveness of this image. It raises the problem of why monastic reality was stylized in this particular direction.

In this chapter, I will make some suggestions—with due hesitation, given the complexity of the evidence—as to why this choice came to be made in Egypt. Finally, by way of a conclusion, I will draw attention to the long-term implications of the choice, and to the manner in which the tensions that came to the surface in the fierce debate in monastic circles on work and its absence came to be resolved in the course in the fifth century AD.

Let us begin, though, by making plain that the choice itself was by no means necessary and inevitable. It cannot be reduced to an ineradicable difference between the ecology of Egypt and that of Syria, as I myself had once imprudently suggested.[1] Egyptian monks did not resort to work because, unlike the steppe lands and mountain foothills of Syria, the desert of Egypt was an unforgiving place, where settlement was possible only through continuous labor. The work of James Goehring has undermined this simple dichotomy. He points out that the monks did not simply vanish into the alien vastness of the Egyptian desert, where they had to work so as to survive. Rather, monastic literature presented the desert as far more remote and forbidding than it was in reality. By treating the desert as a zone that was totally separate from the settled land, monastic writers aimed to keep monks in their place—that is, in a notionally separate desert and out of the settled land. They were declared to belong to the desert. They were expected to stay there. They were headed off from more fertile ecological zones where it would have been quite possible to live the life of a Syrian hermit as a magnetic "stranger"—in the world but not of it.[2]

Still less can the choice of work be reduced to deep-rooted differences of national temperament. Egyptians did not simply work because, being fellahin, they knew of nothing better to do. At the end of the nineteenth century, the great collector of Coptic manuscripts Émile Amélineau was prepared to say (without a trace of embarrassment) that "those coarse fellahin . . . have always been what they are—persons hardened to labor, with brutal instincts, on whom religion and civilization have brought no new [improving] influence."[3]

As we saw in the last chapter, all that we know about the mixed social origins of the early monastic movement in Egypt contradicts this odious opinion.

Altogether we cannot treat Syria and Egypt as if each was an entirely separate world. The problem was that they were intervisible: the practices of the one region would be well known to the other. Instead, we are faced with a war of representations. This war of representations was played out like a great shadow show. Exaggerated figures were thrown across the screen. They should not be allowed to sway our impression of what these monastic landscapes were like in reality: there was always room in both regions for exceptions and for compromises. But the shadow show of ideal images did have a purpose. It conjured up "Syria" and "Egypt" as two poles of the monastic world. It drew attention to a significant choice—to work or not to work. The

TREASURE IN HEAVEN

historian has to estimate the weight of the issues condensed in this choice, and the exact significance that contemporaries attached to that choice.

In order to do this, let us return to a theme that has run throughout this book—that is, to the ancient Christian and Jewish preoccupation with the avoidance of the dependency-generating gift. How could a monk receive gifts without being tarnished by the suspicion that he had succumbed to the love of money? How could he make plain that he had not fallen under an obligation to the giver, as would be expected to happen in a society ruled by rigid laws of reciprocity and dominated, in normal life, by powerful patrons and rich donors? Such patrons and donors were ever present in the Jewish communities, in a manner that exercised the rabbis throughout late antiquity. As we have seen, from the third century onward, they had also come to stay in the Christian churches.

We must remember that, in this, the monks of Egypt were no different from the Christian clergy of earlier centuries or from the rabbis. They were always surrounded by potential donors and patrons. Yet such donors are surprisingly difficult to see in monastic sources. It is as if they had been airbrushed out of the picture. It is important to stress this fact. If the evidence for the monastic movement in Egypt is truly vulnerable to criticism from modern scholars, it is less that it tempts us to accept at face value the exaggerations and carefully constructed self-image of the monks. It is, instead, that we have been led, by the very vividness of the monastic sources, to see the world of the monks in almost total isolation. The monks are made to stand for Christian Egypt as a whole.

What is lacking in our image of Christian Egypt are the Christian churches of the Nile valley. And most lacking of all are the laity who, on the ground, kept these churches going. The world of the local churches and of the laity, who supported both churches and monks, remains the dark side of the moon for the study of Christian Egypt. In order to remedy this lacuna, let us look for a moment at the laity.[4]

The laity are hard to see because much of the recent scholarship on Egyptian monasticism has been devoted exclusively to the relations between monks, bishops, and clergy. We tend to forget that, in many ways, it was the laity who did most to determine the manner in which the monks presented themselves to society at large. For one gifted clerical author, such as Athanasius or Palladius, there were hundreds of laymen and -women whose daily expectations silently molded the image of monks and nuns in Egypt. But these laypersons are dim presences. Like an X-ray which shows bones clearly while the cartilage in which they are enveloped is barely visible, so the laity do not make as vivid an appearance in modern accounts of Egyptian monasticism as do the monks, bishops, and clergy. Yet, in studying monasticism, in Egypt and elsewhere, we should always look out for the constant presence of pious laymen and laywomen.

In order to remedy this defect, it is best to turn to the recent work of Mariachiara Giorda, and especially to her new book, *Il regno di Dio in terra*. This book makes plain the extent to which monasticism (in Egypt as elsewhere) was an overwhelmingly lay movement.[5] It recruited most of its adherents from the laity. Its successes were watched with intent eyes by the laity.

Why was this so? Put very briefly: the monks brought to the laity of Egypt what lay Christians (and, indeed, most religious persons in late antiquity) had always wanted. They brought access to the holy—in this case, through persons touched by the hand of God. One of the very first allusions to a monk comes from a papyrus of around 340. In it, the Lady Valeria wrote to an otherwise unknown ascetic, Paphnutius:

> I ask and exhort you, most honored father, that you request for me [help] from Christ that I may receive healing; I believe that in this way through your prayers I am receiving healing, for to those who are ascetics and religious revelations are shown. For I am overcome with a serious disease in the form of a terrible difficulty in breathing. . . . Even though in body I have not come to your feet, yet in spirit I have come to your feet.[6]

It is a striking voice from the past. We should pay attention to it. A strong case has recently been made, by Peter van Minnen and others, that we should not exaggerate the role of monastic holy men and of thaumaturgic activity in the growth of Egyptian Christianity.[7] Van Minnen reminds us that the holy persons of monastic origin (monks and nuns alike) remained overshadowed, in the Egyptian religious imagination, by the legends of the martyrs, whose shrines had sprung up in towns and villages all over the settled land.[8] There is much truth in this view. Nevertheless, we should not overlook the expectations of advice, healing, and blessing which drew potential donors to the monks.

Valeria was not alone. Letters addressed by Paul, a layman detained by business in Alexandria, and by a lady called Tapiam, to Nepheros, a priest with the reputation of being a holy man, show a similar pattern.[9] Nepheros was approached as a "man of God."[10] His prayers were believed to act as "nourishment for the soul along the way and as grounds for hope in the world to come."[11] Other priests addressed Nepheros as "Your Sweet Perfume."[12] We do not know whether Valeria sent gifts to Paphnutios. But Paul certainly went out of his way to forward a great jar of oil to Nepheros, much as the Lady Eirene had sent oil to the Manichaean Elect.[13] If Peter van Minnen had told these persons, "We need to resist making the past more charismatic than it was,"[14] I think that they would have been sadly disappointed.

"If You Are Giving It to God . . . Then Be Quiet"

The Lady Valeria, the correspondents of the priest Nepheros, and the Lady Eirene, who supported the Manichaean Elect in distant Kellis, were exact contemporaries. They all inhabited a religious landscape where individual holy persons were believed to be able to open the door to the other world. But each group handled in a different manner the nature of the bond established between the holy persons (or group of persons) and their petitioners.

The Manichaean Elect accepted the gifts of food and shelter from their laity in a splendidly *de haut en bas* manner. Their vision of a fallen cosmos persuaded them and their admirers that the mighty prayers of the Elect alone were more than enough return to the Lady Eirene for her great jars of oil. The Elect already belonged to the other world to such a degree that gifts were not problematic for them. With figures whose relationship with their donors was so ethereal and so highly ritualized, gifts generated no dependency.

Not so the monks of Egypt. It is significant that the monks, though contemporaries and neighbors of the Manichees, went out of their way to avoid that high-pitched solution. They appealed to another imaginative pattern. That was an image of the independent man that was firmly ensconced in the classical tradition. Their pointedly pared-down lifestyle and constant work patterns projected an ideal of autarky that was common among the farmers of the Mediterranean. Indeed, it was an ideal that was all the more esteemed in principle for being seldom realized in practice.[15]

Nor was autarky an ideal limited to peasants. Philosophers owed no small part of their authority in Roman culture and politics to the fact that they were believed to have adopted an autarkic lifestyle. Though many philosophers remained rich, they were considered to have managed their affairs with such exemplary restraint that they could be trusted to be above money. Such was the philosopher Musonius Rufus, the "Roman Socrates" of the first century AD. Musonius even recommended that a philosopher should work on his own farm—though he was not to undertake anything too hard! He advised his charges that such humble work would inspire them to "endure hardships and . . . the pains of labor, rather than depend upon another for sustenance."[16] Above all, the weight of the gift would not sway their judgment. Even in the Talmud, an uncorrupt Roman governor was called a *philosophos*—a true philosopher. For "he bore a reputation that he did not accept bribes."[17]

In the monastic circles encouraged by Athanasius and reported upon by Palladius and others, the "work of the hands" came to bear a quite unusual weight of meaning for the same reason. It marked out the monks as autarkic persons. They were self-supporting. Therefore, they were above money.

The dogged display of self-sufficiency by the monks altered

the way in which gifts to them were perceived. Monks had paid their dues. They could feed themselves. They were not in it for the money. They proved this by appearing as constant workers, untouched by idleness. Just as important, those who gave to them were reassured that they were giving to truly detached persons, unmoved by avarice.

This was particularly important for the monks of the fourth century. At that time, monasticism in Egypt was an economically fragile institution. However organized (whether as hermits, in loose confederacies of cells—the *laurai*—or in monasteries proper), monks were seldom if ever able to make ends meet. The skills privileged by monastic literature were not moneymakers. Monasteries were full of elderly monks and young children. It was often difficult for them to turn out an effective workforce.[18] In the words of Apa Serinos: "I have spent my time being a harvest laborer, on sewing, on plaiting [basketwork]. And in all of these, if the hand of God had not fed me, I could not have fed myself."[19]

By the "hand of God" Serinos meant, quite simply, the gifts to monks by nonmonks (clergy or laity). It was the hand of God's providence which joined the hands of pious donors to the hands of the monks through the occasional, providential gift. Hence a paradox. The insistence of the monks of Egypt on an ideal of autarky based on the "work of the hands" created a situation where monks were rarely able to achieve economic independence. Even when they drew on "undisclosed" income, such as rents or the profits of weaving (activities that were held to be less consonant with a monastic lifestyle, and for that reason appear rarely in monastic sources), they still needed gifts in order to survive.

Altogether, the monastic movement in Egypt was kept afloat through the generosity of pious laypersons. Yet we only occasionally get a glimpse of this situation. In the vicinity of Scetis, the pious laywoman Taësia was said to have bankrupted herself in supporting the neighboring monks. She was forced to turn to prostitution (thus becoming the model—the very distant model!—for Anatole France's novel *Thaïs*). When monks from Scetis visited her high-class brothel in an attempt to reclaim her, the concierge told them, "You monks, from the very beginning, have devoured her wealth."[20] A pagan critic of the monks could not have put it more bluntly.

With considerable aplomb, those who wrote about the monks turned the problem into the solution. Though insufficient in itself to keep them afloat, the monks' working with their own hands gave out a strong message of self-sufficiency. As long as they worked and were seen to work, monks were eligible to receive the discreet but ever-present flow of money that lay admirers were quite prepared to lavish on them as teachers, diviners, miracle workers, and advisers.

But there was more to it than avoiding a reputation for idleness and greed. Great monks emerged as the enablers of the most precious form of giving to the holy—the utterly free gift to God, with no strings attached. The silent and impassive gaze of a monk, whose reputation for self-sufficiency ensured that he could be considered to be immune to the normal pull of avarice, sped the earthly treasure provided by donors on its way to an imagined treasure house, somewhere in the silence of the other world. Proud of the fact that they themselves needed nothing, because they could fend for themselves by the "work of the hands," the monks were the perfect nonreceivers. Their detachment from the gifts that they received echoed the vast and benevolent detachment of God himself.

In his *Lausiac History*, Palladius presented a vivid portrait of the great Apa Pambo in action as a model nonreceiver. On one occasion, Pambo was visited by Melania the Elder, a senatorial lady from old Rome. Melania was so grand that the Coptic version of the *History* referred to her as "Melania, the Queen of the Romans." Palladius described their memorable encounter.

> The blessed Melania told me this: "When I first came from Rome to Alexandria . . . I took [to Pambo] a silver coffer containing three hundred pounds of coins. He was sitting weaving palm leaves, and he merely blessed me and said: 'May God reward you!'"
>
> And he told his steward Origen: "Take this and dispense it

TREASURE IN HEAVEN

to all the brethren down in [distant] Libya, and on the islands, for those monasteries are in greater need."

[Somewhat upset by Pambo's studied indifference, Melania continued] . . . "So you may know, O lord, how much it is, there are three hundred pounds."

[Pambo] did not so much as raise his head, but said: "My child, He who measures the mountains knows better the amount of silver. If you were giving it to me, you spoke well; but if you are giving it to God, who did not overlook the two small coins [of the widow, who gave to the treasury of the Temple, in Mark 12:42 and Luke 21:1–4], then be quiet."[21]

The narratives of the desert monks are full of stories of gift exchanges that were as solemn as a Japanese tea ceremony. Passing on from Pambo to visit the cell of Macarius of Alexandria, Melania received from him the fleece of a ram "as a host's gift to a guest." By reciprocating the gifts that must have accompanied the great lady's visit with a gift of his own, Macarius came out equal. He too was an independent man. He too had gifts to give. Furthermore, what he gave was no ordinary fleece. It had been brought to Macarius by a grateful hyena, whose cub he had cured of blindness. The hyena stood for the model layperson, playing her role in an exchange where the spiritual gift of healing was met by a material countergift.[22] Now Macarius gave the fleece to Melania, as a vivid countergift in return for her support.

The spiritual exchanges between monks and laypersons that are described in the monastic literature of Egypt were just as intense, and, in many ways, as one-sided, as the one-sided giving that bound devotees to more "angelic" persons (such as the Manichaean Elect). But, unlike the Manichees and Syrians, the Egyptian monks followed patterns recognizably similar to those which bound normal human beings to each other through mutual giving in the lay world—like normal householders they extended hospitality to visitors and made sure that they did not leave without carrying away with them some concrete countergift, even if it was no more than a sieve, a basket, or a fleece. For all their miraculous shimmer, by insisting on a normal exchange of material gifts for material gifts, monks carried with them the reassuring smell of humanity.

"You Are a Human Being . . . You Must Work . . . in Order to Eat"

For this reason, I would suggest that the symbolic role of the "work of the hands" practiced by the monks of Egypt was heightened by a further consideration. In Egypt, work was always something more than a guarantee of the monastic virtue of financial independence. Labor in itself was treated as a charged denotator of the humanity which the monks claimed to share with all fellow Christians—indeed, with all human beings.

As we have seen, in the Syrian tradition, to escape the drudgery, the *ponos*, the *'amla*, of labor was to enter the charmed world of the angels. It was to transcend a humanity defined by the ancient curse of work. As the humorous account of the attempt of the young John the Dwarf to become an instant angel through knocking off work makes plain, this view was not shared by the compilers of the *Sayings of the Desert Fathers*. The crestfallen John was rebuked by his companion: "You are a human being . . . you must work . . . in order to eat."[23]

This exchange between John and his fellow monk was more than a quaint anecdote. It was an integral part of the image of the monk. An Egyptian monk was not an angel. By the fifth century, this image had seeped into lay circles all over Egypt. At first sight, one would not expect monks to be mentioned by the Neoplatonist philosopher and eventual bishop of Ptolemais, Synesius of Cyrene (370–414). Synesius had been a pupil of none other than the pagan woman philosopher Hypatia, whose brutal lynching by a Christian mob at the instigation of the patriarch Cyril of Alexandria, in 415, stood for all that pagans (and modern persons) detested about the rise of Christianity. Yet monks made a cameo appearance in the works of Synesius. In around 403, in his tract entitled *On Dio* [Dio Chrysostom] *and Life as Lived according to His Example*, Synesius attacked the views of extreme mystics who thought that they could reach ecstatic communion with God without the slow labor of the mind associated with Greek philosophy. They thought that they could reach God "as if in a Bacchic frenzy, like the leap of a man mad or possessed." To remind these persons that they should remember that they were only human, Synesius turned to the example of the monks: "They know that they are but men. . . . What, after all, is the meaning of their baskets and of the wickerwork objects that they handle, if not to signify first of all that they were human beings?"[24]

To work was to be human. It is here, I suggest—that is, in the realm of long-term patterns of the social imagination—that Egypt may well have differed for millennia from the world of Syria. From the very beginning of its history, Egypt was unlike Syria when it came to the matter of work. Ancient Egyptians do not seem to have been haunted by potent myths of the loss of leisure in the way that the populations of the Fertile Crescent had been, since the days of the great *Atrahasis* myth and the proverbs of ancient Sumer. For ancient Egyptians, the fact of work did not stir memories of a social trauma at the dawn of time. It was not seen as a degrading condition that only a few exceptional human beings might be enabled to transcend. Labor was not problematized. It is no coincidence that the funerary art of Pharaonic times provides an exceptional body of material (painted tombs and innumerable little models of servants of every kind) that illustrates, with loving circumstantiality, every aspect of labor in the ancient Near East.[25]

Of course, the privileged few did not participate in this labor. They directed it, both in this world and in the next. Like the great rentiers of fourth-century Antioch, the Pharaohs and their aristocracy were great believers in *ponos* . . . for others. But even they saw nothing demeaning about being portrayed in the Field of Reeds of the Other World—the Egyptian Elysian Fields— lending a hand with the harvest. Such was the case of the aristocrat Sennedjem—Mr. Pleasant—and his wife, in the noble graves of Deir el-Madina of 1280 BC.[26] Altogether, work was not banished from Paradise. It was not a curse. Both in this world and in the next, it was accepted as an integral part of the human condition.

Rather, the true, deep trauma that weighed upon the collective memory of Egypt was not work: it was famine.[27] At any time, the rains that swept across equatorial Africa to pour in torrents from the high mountains of Ethiopia into the sources of the Nile might fail. And, if the flood did not rise, the land died, and the people with it—horribly and in tens of thousands. From the earliest times, Egyptians recorded these years of "distress," of which the seven "lean" years of the story of Joseph in Egypt in the book of Genesis were a distant and cosmeticized echo.[28]

Such times of distress were all the more traumatic because they were infrequent and unpredictable. Each incident stood out in high relief. Furthermore, they fell on a countryside that lacked the wide margins of land (steppe, mountainside, and swamp) from which famine foods could be gathered, as was the case in the rest of the Mediterranean.[29] It was not only the failure of the rains of equatorial Africa that could cause this disaster. In times of political unrest the neglect of the irrigation works that controlled the flooding of the Nile would lead to similar lethal shortages.[30]

Hence the tenacity with which Egyptians, living under the shadow of famine, identified bread with life. That this bread also cost work mattered far less to them than the fact that its absence spelled death. The great local lords of earlier times had boasted that they had "fed" their city with bread from their own warehouses. Later, the Pharaohs came to be acclaimed as the predominant "nourishers" of Egypt.[31] But, whoever provided the bread, bread was life; and those without access to bread were thought to tremble on the edge of annihilation.

Thus, the absence of bread—and not the presence of toil—was the surest mark of poverty. Only in a topsy-turvy world, according to the *Prophecy of Neferti* (from the second millennium BC), would beggars amass riches and the poor "eat their fill of bread."[32] Such patterns of the social imagination had lasted into late antiquity. In the Coptic language, the word for "poor"—*ḥéke*—and the word for hunger—*ḥko*—derived directly from the ancient Egyptian, *ḥqr*—to be hungry.[33]

These fears were still ever present in the Egypt of the fourth

TREASURE IN HEAVEN

century. It was remembered, at a time of famine, that Pachomius "also prayed to the Lord with great insistence to cause the level of the waters to rise to a good height so that abundance might prevail on the earth and that men find bread, eat, live and bless the Lord."[34]

"Can God Spread a Table in the Wilderness?": Food and the Desert in the *Historia Monachorum*

Foreign visitors to the monasteries of Middle Egypt quickly picked up the basic building blocks of the social imagination of a land that accepted labor, but that always yearned fiercely for bread. The *Historia Monachorum in Aegypto*—the *Travelogue of the Monks in Egypt*—was written in the early 390s for a community in Jerusalem. It has often been treated as a work of mere make-believe that throws more light on the mentality of the writers than on the reality of the Egyptian desert.[35] But this, I think, is to underestimate the extent to which the monastic travelers, as they made their way up the Nile from Palestine, were dependent on local informants.

These local informants passed on to them what students of social memory (I think especially of the lucid little book *Social Memory* by James Fentress and Chris Wickham) call "oikotypes." Oikotypes are memories that fit well into the general expectations of a given society. For this reason, they are easily remembered and enjoy a longer shelf life than do tales that seem too strange, too bizarre, too unaccustomed, to be lodged in the memory of a region.[36]

The "oikotypical" tales that the visiting monks brought back with them from Egypt were, to an extraordinary degree, tales about food. First: there were tales of abundance. Sand blessed by Apa Copres turned into the most fertile ground in Egypt.[37] Apa Hellé told his visitors how peasants would come with baskets and scoop up the sand on which the holy man's feet had trodden, so as to scatter it on their gardens.[38] To the author of the *Historia Monachorum* these were "true" miracles. For, in them, it was not only human bodies that were healed (a thing which even doctors could do). Nature itself was cured. It recovered its natural abundance.[39]

Myths of abundance hovered at the edge of the narrative of the *Historia Monachorum.* Apa Apollonius explained to visitors why the population of Egypt worshipped vegetables. They did this because their tenacious attachment to the land had once saved them from disaster. At the time of the exodus of the people of Israel from Egypt, the majority of the Egyptians had decided to stay at home to tend their fields. They did not follow Pharaoh in pursuit of the Israelites. Thus, they avoided being drowned along with Pharaoh and his army in the waters of the Red Sea. Ever since, said Apa Apollonius, they had paid grateful homage to garden herbs.[40]

But the *Historia Monachorum* contained more unearthly stories. These stories assumed a distinctive imaginative geography, which Dimitrios Moschos has called a *spatiale Jenseits*—a spatialized Other World.[41] The stages of any journey into this spatialized Other World were marked out in terms of differing zones of food, each of which required differing degrees of labor.[42] Monks who reached the deepest desert came closest to God. They would be reminded of His presence by the appearance, often at the head of the cloak on which they slept, of warm loaves of the purest flour. These mysterious loaves were a reminder that God had, indeed, met the challenge of the children of Israel in Sinai (in Psalm 78:19): *"Can God spread a table in the wilderness?"*[43]

Furthermore, somewhere beyond the dead sands of the desert, there lay the garden of Eden. A hardy monk, Patermuthius, had once made the journey to that place of magical abundance. He had brought back with him a giant fig so sweet that the very smell of it would heal the sick.[44] On another occasion, a group of monks were visited at the end of their fast by a young man who bore honeycombs, a jar of milk, and enormous dates, along with "warm fresh bread as if from a foreign land."[45] Most poignant of all, at the touch of famine, the peasants of the region would flock to the large monastery of Apa Apollo in the neighborhood of Hermopolis, believing that the monks were fed *amékhanôs*—without human devices—from heaven itself.[46]

TREASURE IN HEAVEN

But the most vivid story of all in the *Historia Monachorum* was an eerie one. It showed how, in this spatialized Other World, the boundaries between the human and the nonhuman were delineated, as on a great map that spread from the lush green of the Nile valley to the inner desert, in terms of the availability of food. A monk who lived in the inner desert found that bread would appear from nowhere on his table every two or three days. But, over time, this sure supply of bread made his ascetic ardor cool. A barely perceptible inertia began to make its way into his soul. As this inertia spread, the quality of the bread declined. At the end, the monk found only a mouse-eaten crust. A monastic Dorian Gray, he knew that his soul was no longer worthy of the desert, the zone of God-given food. He made his way back to a monastery on the edge of the green land of the Nile. He joined his fellows. He returned to his handiwork. He had learned what it was to be human. To be human, in Egypt, was to depend on human bread, produced by human labor, and purchased through the sale to fellow humans of the work of human hands.[47]

It was with these vivid stories—stories that linked food and labor with being human—at the back of their minds that the monks of Egypt countered the Syrian myth of an "angelic" freedom gained through the abandonment of the world of labor.

"A Complete Equality Will Come About": Monks, Clergy, and the Care of the Poor

Last, but by no means least, the current image of the monk—and also of the nun—left room also for the care of the poor. Along with the shared pull of the belly, awareness of the duty to work so as to provide for the poor, like any other good Christian householder, anchored the heart of the monk to humanity.

One should add that it also eased the relations of monks and nuns with the neighboring clergy. In the conditions of the fourth century, this was necessary. Exclusive concentration on monastic sources alone makes us forget that profound changes were under way in the Christian churches of Egypt as a whole. Both in towns and in villages, the process of *ordo* building, which, as we have seen, was already a prominent feature of the Christianity of the third-century Mediterranean, was in full spate. By 439, the village of Karanis (which was not necessarily a very prosperous village) could produce seventeen clerics at a meeting to settle a dispute over irrigation.[48] Proud men, settling into roles of leadership in hitherto somewhat "rudderless" villages,[49] the clergy were a new nomenklatura.

Such men were unlikely to tolerate monks and nuns who, as the recipients of gifts, lured potential donors away from supporting their own churches. Such a conflict on the ground for scarce resources between two groups of fund-raisers could be bitter and protracted. It was considerably more likely to provoke tension between monks and clergy than was any supposed conflict between "charismatic" monks and an "institutional" church. Such a conflict between the "charismatic" and the "institutional" has been imposed upon the history of the monastic movement, in Egypt and elsewhere, by modern religious historians influenced by Max Weber. In fourth-century Egypt, however, bishops and priests did not read Max Weber. But they kept a close eye on their income from offerings by the faithful. They did not wish these offerings to be diminished by competitors.

Yet the evidence for this competition is virtually nonexistent. One suspects that monastic sources studiously avoided mentioning such incidents if they occurred. But conflicts over offerings between holy men and the local clergy appear in both Syria and Asia Minor.[50] What was it in Egypt that took the pressure off a potentially bitter zero-sum game? I would suggest that it was a lacuna in the organization of the churches themselves, to which Ewa Wipszycka has recently drawn attention.

Writing on the charitable activities of bishops in Egypt, Wipszycka reported that she found, somewhat to her surprise, that the local churches had no organized system for the care of the poor. The offerings of the faithful were absorbed by the salaries of the clergy and by the upkeep of the church and its furnishings. Some churches were little oases of splendor, filled with silver vessels, great candelabra, and heavy silken veils.[51] Unless provided for by rich founders, the cost of their maintenance would soon

       TREASURE IN HEAVEN

have swallowed up any leftover surplus that might have gone to the poor. As a result, only the bishop was in a position to give alms on a regular basis. And the bishop could be a long way away. Hence, in much of the countryside of Egypt, it was left to the monks to take up the slack in organized almsgiving to the poor.

This does not mean that every monastery and settlement of hermits was a center of poor relief. Far from it. Many monks used their surpluses to minister only to the needs of their fellow monks, incapacitated by illness and old age. In the words of John the Dwarf: "My widows and orphans are in Scetis [that is, in the large monastic settlement to which John belonged]."[52]

Nonetheless, to represent the monk as a peculiar kind of Christian householder gave the Christian poor a lever on his heart. Monks and nuns could be approached as a source of alms. Furthermore, monks came to play a role in encouraging lay giving to the poor. The fifth-century saint Matthew the Poor was imagined to have done this.

It was said that Matthew always stood at the gate of his monastery. He was constantly giving to the poor. He also urged rich visitors to the monastery to join with him. To encourage them, Matthew quoted the famous verses of Saint Paul. Paul had promised to the community as a whole a miraculous abundance that would be as great and as equally distributed as the abundance of the holy manna that had once fallen on the children of Israel in the desert of Sinai (2 Cor. 8:14–15).[53] Matthew insisted that similar abundance would be set loose by the rich, if only they were generous to the poor: "Christ has chosen you to be his estate managers, [he told them] so that you can give to the needy. For then a complete equality [shôsh ñouôt] will come about for all mankind."

In citing Paul in this way, Matthew was appealing to a utopian notion. Paul had promised a complete isotés—an equality of wealth. By this he meant that wealth would come to be spread equally throughout the federation of Christian communities: those who gave to Paul's collection would eventually benefit from a similar collection. Wealth would level up between the different churches, like the miraculous leveling up of all portions of the manna that had fallen from heaven upon the children of Israel.[54] Matthew used this image to promise a similar leveling up between the rich and the local poor through almsgiving at his monastery.

But Matthew also was sensitive to the difference between the poor and the "holy poor." Gifts to the holy poor—the monks—were a serious matter. When a widow reneged on her promise to offer a boat to the monastery, Matthew prayed—and the boat was swallowed up in a whirlpool in the Nile.[55]

It was the common interest of monks and clergymen in donations and the common need to provide for the local poor that may have drawn monks and clergy together, thereby accelerating the process (well described by Mariachiara Giorda) by which, in the fifth and sixth centuries, clergy and monks merged to form a single privileged group, separate from the laity and each equally entitled to a share of lay offerings.[56]

"Neither Shall I Eat While My Fellow-Members [in Christ] Go Hungry": The Body, Compassion, and the Poor

And yet there may be more to it than that. In Egypt, monastic thinkers and preachers of the time were more than usually preoccupied with what it was to be "human." For them, to be "human" was to have a body. This body had to be fed and clothed. Hence the insistence, in the monastic stories that we have studied, that a monk could not claim to be an angel. He was to work because he was human and had the needs of a human body. But to be human also meant to be aware that one had a body in common with other humans. This included a sense of kinship with the endangered bodies of the poor. Compassion for the poor was not a mere sentiment. It was seen to be an almost visceral reaction to the suffering of common flesh. "Apa Agathon would say: 'If I could meet a beggar, give him my body and take his, I should be very happy.' That, indeed, is perfect charity."[57]

Egyptian monastic piety insisted on this bond of common flesh. Hence the intensity with which the Egyptian theologians who inspired the monks (beginning with the great Athanasius of Alexandria) came to focus on the Incarnation. Through the Incarnation, Christ had become human. This meant that he had come to share human flesh. Christ's physical suffering was all the more awesome for having been endured by a god. But the sufferings that Christ endured were the same as those endured by any other human being. Christ's sufferings were our sufferings. Contemplation of the one was supposed to lead to heightened compassion for the other.

This theological insistence that Christ had shared in the sufferings of humanity was supposed to have practical results. In his letters to the great, Shenoute of Atripe told them that he would read the story of the Crucifixion of Christ with tears rolling down his cheeks. In the same letters, he urged judges, governors, and great landowners to feel the same degree of compassion for the poor as they would feel for the suffering Christ. He reminded them that the poor endured every day what Christ had suffered. Furthermore, the poor suffered in bodies that were the same as those of the rich and powerful.[58] To ignore the body was to ignore the bonds that tied one, subliminally but tenaciously, to the poor.

This streak of physicality was marked in Egypt. A respect for the integrity of the body seems to have survived from ancient times. It has even been argued by some that mummification continued largely unchanged in Christian circles.[59] Scholars of Coptic Egypt have been struck by the manner in which legends of the Egyptian martyrs stressed the fact that their bodies had miraculously resisted dismemberment, both before and after death. The saints often lay above ground in their shrines as if mummified. Their bodies were gloriously intact.[60]

Although direct continuities with ancient Egyptian practice may be more apparent than real, it appears that a similar emphasis on the integrity of the body characterized fourth- and fifth-century debates on the Resurrection in monastic circles in Egypt. Such debates were by no means limited to Egypt. But it is revealing that the Egyptian monks came down heavily on the side of a literal, physical resurrection of the flesh. Human beings would remain human. They would never be transformed, beyond recognition, into ethereal, angelic beings. The body could never be left behind. Without a body, the soul was incomplete. It was "like a singer who had lost his voice."[61]

These debates have recently been studied with exemplary erudition by Dimitrij Bumazhnov and by Paul Patterson.[62] The Egyptian consensus that emerged from such debates was that to be human was to be tied to the body. Alternative views, which promised to think away the body so as to achieve an "angelic" state, were roundly condemned. As far as a monk's links to society were concerned, this meant that to accept the body was to abandon any pretense to be an angel. It involved taking on work so as to feed the body. It also involved taking on the poor, so as to show compassion for bodies like one's own.

These debates go some way to explain Pachomius's prayers for the rising of the Nile in a time of famine. These prayers showed a concern for all Egypt as it faced famine, the primal fear of all Egyptians since ancient times. Furthermore, the fasts that Pachomius undertook at that time showed that he wished to feel the sufferings of the victims in his own body. His fast was explicitly presented, in the *Bohairic [Coptic] Life of Pachomius*, as a fast that linked the great abbot to the poor: "Neither shall I eat while my fellow-members [in Christ] go hungry and find no bread to eat."[63] It was in these many ways—some practical, some austerely theological—that work, humanity, and compassion for the poor came together in the worldview of the monks of Egypt.

Conclusion

The End of an Era

It is tempting to end on these noble words of Pachomius. But the historian has to go on to ask, What happened next? The short, conventional answer is that things quieted down. We tend to forget what an unusual century the fourth century had been. In her brilliant study of 1977, *Pauvreté économique et pauvreté sociale à Byzance* (a book that is still the most thrilling analysis ever written of late Roman society seen from the viewpoint of the poor and, by implication, of the monks), Évelyne Patlagean has rightly spoken of the "strange, short-lived freedom that gripped the Roman world of the fourth century in the interval between two civilizations."[1]

A significant aspect of the more stable early Byzantine civilization that emerged in the course of the fifth and sixth centuries was a closing down of ascetic options and a consequent regularization of the monastic life. Many scholars have attempted to do justice to this change. The tendency has been to see it in terms of the growing strength of the institutional church. Such an opinion derives its narrative cogency from a view of the sociology of early Christianity propounded under the aegis of Max Weber. This view stresses the supposed conflict between charisma and office—between monks (as representing charismatic power) and bishops (as representing the power of an institution).

Seen in this light, the story of the post-fourth-century world is the story of the decline of charisma and the rise of a more institutionalized Christianity. It is usually told as a sad story. It has proved hard to resist seeing the more colorful movements and figures of the fourth and early fifth centuries as the last of their kind—as the representatives of a more free and charismatic Christianity that was doomed to give way to a uniform and hierarchical established church.

But this view makes history happen too fast and in a single direction. For example, the "angelic" life of the holy men of Syria (such as I described it in our third and fourth chapters) was by no means condemned to obsolescence, despite its charismatic aspects. Holy men in the Syrian tradition remained prominent throughout the fifth and sixth centuries. They were not simply bizarre reminders of a form of Christianity condemned by history (as written by church historians under the influence of Max Weber) to extinction. As we have seen, the lifestyle of these "angelic" persons was based on deeply meditated views on the nature of the human person and of society. These views were there to stay.

In AD 500, for instance, a holy man set up a tent outside the long-deserted imperial palace at Antioch. Wearing only one tunic, he was fed by a pious fuller, who bought his hero's food out of his own wages. There was no hint of the "work of the hands" in the life of this Syrian holy man. His life was devoted exclusively to prayer. "In this way, he served as a model for the whole world . . . and had been sent [by God] as a sign."[2]

Nor should we exaggerate the success of the episcopate in bringing the monks to heel. The decrees of the Council of Chalcedon of 451 are held, by many scholars, to mark the end of an epoch of monastic freedom. In these decrees, the council ruled that all monasteries were to be under the supervision of the local bishop.[3] But one can doubt whether these regulations were enforced by all bishops in all regions.[4] The slowness with which many of the reforms of the Council of Trent were implemented in the considerably more compact and tightly governed world of sixteenth-century Europe would lead me to doubt that the decrees of the Council of Chalcedon were imposed with any greater success.[5]

Altogether, divergent styles of ascetic life were neither put out of date nor suppressed. Nothing shows this more clearly than

TREASURE IN HEAVEN

does the situation in Syria. Here a spate of building covered the landscape with monasteries. The remarkable survey by Lukas Schachner of the mountain regions of northern Syria (especially the Limestone Massif, the Jebel al-'Alâ, and the Jebel Barisha) shows monasteries thick on the ground. There was a monastery every four square kilometers. None were farther away from the villages than eight hundred meters. Far from being worlds set apart, monasteries were closely woven into the economic life of the region.[6] Yet we do not know whether the monks in them worked. Many may have been rentiers, living lives devoted only to prayer.[7]

Many of these sites were dominated by a tower in which Stylite hermits (imitators of the "angelic" life of the great Symeon) lodged. Some were complete with balconies from which these angelic figures dispensed preaching and blessing in return for material support from the laity. By the year 500, the towers and pillars of Stylites had achieved "enormous visibility" (to use the words of Schachner) all over the hills of northern Syria.[8] This bristling horizon showed that the "angelic" life was still alive and well.

With the passing of time, the Syrians came to accept a "mixed economy" in monastic lifestyles. Versions of the Egyptian model came to be widely accepted.[9] Many centuries later, in the 770s, the great Syriac spiritual writer Joseph Hazzaya ("the Seeing One") looked back on the differences between Syria and Egypt, when writing to the head of a Syrian monastery. He was well aware of the divergence between the two regions. He even cited the famous anecdote about John the Dwarf from the *Sayings of the Desert Fathers*. He agreed that a young monk had no right to abandon work so as to become an instant angel.[10] He also agreed that a monk should work so as to make himself independent of donors. He even went on to add that a self-supporting monk would not be disturbed to such an extent by the stream of peasants (men and women alike) who were in the habit of visiting workless monks with little gifts of food and other necessaries, in return for blessing, advice—and the chance of a good gossip.

Yet Joseph remained loyal to the core of the Syrian tradition. Work was for young monks and for those who "are below perfection."

"But those who have reached the spiritual stage have no need of this, because, even if the things necessary for their needs are produced by others, no harm is done to them."[11]

The blending of the traditions of the two regions had begun much earlier. Even by the time of Philoxenos of Mabbûg, in the 520s, the hard outlines of the Syrian model of a binary community based on the contrast between the lives of the Perfect and the lives of the Upright (such as was described in the *Book of Steps*) had softened. In the words of Robert Kitchen, for Philoxenos the two lifestyles (the Perfect and the Upright) had evolved "from almost mutually exclusive ways of life to an open-ended continuum."[12]

"The Storehouse of Blessing": New Wealth and New Patrons

We should perhaps look in a different direction to explain the general reduction of tension between the varying forms of asceticism in eastern Christianity. I would suggest that what may have changed slowly but irreversibly in this period was the attitude of the laity to the wealth of the church in general and to wealth given to monks in particular. We are entering a more euphoric age of church finances. In all provinces of the East (both in Egypt and in Syria), churches and monasteries alike rose slowly but surely on a mounting tide of donations.[13]

This was a new situation. As we have seen, in the less wealthy churches of the late third and fourth centuries, sharp distinctions still needed to be made as to the entitlement to support of different groups or persons. These distinctions were based on a nagging sense, among relatively poor laypersons, that giving was a zero-sum game. What went to some groups could not go to others. Hence a continued debate as to who should receive funds and on what terms—the real poor or the "holy poor"? Monks who worked, or monks who did not work?

In the course of the fifth century, the entry into the churches of truly wealthy patrons and the general prosperity that spread throughout the Middle East and Egypt may have eased these anxieties. It was agreed that those who gave to the church gave to God in the first place, and that God could be trusted to distribute this wealth to the various, potentially competing groups who claimed to benefit from it. The general assumption was that there was enough to go around. In the words of a seventh-century text, the *Questions of Theodore:* "Do not say to yourself, 'I am giving to the priests.' No. You are giving to Jesus, and Jesus will give to the priests."[14]

Whatever the realities on the ground, such a view reflected a novel ease with wealth. All wealth was a "blessing" from God; and, so, why should not the church as a whole—both the clergy and the monks—have its full share of this blessing?

This change has been studied with great sensitivity by Daniel Caner in the monastic literature of the fifth and sixth centuries.[15] Caner's insights have now been applied with great success to the case of Egypt by Ariel López in his outstanding study of Shenoute of Atripe.[16]

López shows that the anxious concerns of an earlier age were swallowed up in the golden glow of a new Christian myth of abundance. He adduces one outstanding example of this new attitude. The church that Shenoute constructed at the great White Monastery near Sohag (in around 440) was "the biggest monastic church built in the Mediterranean world during the late antique period. . . . This was true wealth."[17] It was wealth that cried out to be mystified. Indeed, the wealth needed to build this stupendous structure was supposed to have had a mysterious origin. It was said to have come to Shenoute from a buried treasure miraculously discovered in the sands of the desert.[18] In fact, the cost of the building was met by the rallying of an entire governmental elite (the emperor, perhaps, included). These prominent lay figures were determined to pour money as never before into a major monastery and pilgrimage shrine. Divine Providence had inspired them to bring the "blessing" of wealth to Shenoute's great monastery.[19]

Such huge wealth had not previously been made available for

any church in Upper Egypt. For his part, Shenoute accepted so much heavy-handed patronage by the great because he saw it as coming from the hand of God alone. He no longer had to fear the dependency-generating gift. As abbot of a great complex of monasteries, he was the equal of any lay patron. He could accept the gifts of the rich and powerful without incurring suspicions of subservience or of greed.

On one occasion, none other than Saint Paul appeared to Shenoute in a vision. Paul appeared at a time when Shenoute's monks were anxious that the resources of the monastery might be exhausted by feeding the victims of a famine. Paul's message was reassuring. Shenoute did not have to worry. Abundance would trigger abundance: "Because you love charity and give alms to anyone who asks . . . Behold the Lord has sent me to you to comfort you because of what you have done for the poor."[20] Then Paul handed Shenoute a blessed loaf, which he placed in the monastery's storehouse. From then onward, the supplies for the poor never ran out, and the storehouse came to be known as "The Storehouse of Blessing."[21] "And [Paul] stayed talking with Shenoute until it was time to assemble in the church at night."[22] One wonders what they would have had to say to each other— the missionary fund-raiser of the first century AD, living under the perpetual shadow of the suspicion that he was a trickster; the abbot of a great monastery of the fifth century, as solid as a Pharaonic temple and as colorful as any palace, confident in the resources made available to him by the elites of a Christian empire.

"Lands of the Begging Bowl": Asia, Egypt, and Europe

Finally: what does all this amount to? We should not overlook the long-term implications of the divergence between the "angelic" life of the monks of Syria and of the Manichees and the distinctive lifestyle represented by the laborious monks of Egypt. As we have seen, this divergence was in many ways largely notional. Yet it pointed to significant alternatives. If we overlook it, it is because we tend to take the monks of Egypt for granted. We have become only too used to the image of the Egyptian monk, permanently settled in his monastery, like a holy kibbutznik. It was this image which was first passed on to the Latin world by Jerome in Rome, by Augustine in Hippo and Carthage, and by John Cassian in Marseilles. This image, in turn, deeply influenced the *Rule of Saint Benedict*, which was drawn up for his monastery in southern Italy in the early sixth century.

In later centuries, through the spread of the *Rule of Saint Benedict*, this version of monasticism became the model for the entire Christian West. It is only along the edges of the western monastic tradition that memories of "angelic"—of work-free, begging—monks continued to flicker like summer lightning, until the radical movements of the High Middle Ages threw up disturbing avatars of Syria in the "Perfect" of the Cathars and in the early Franciscans. Despite these exceptions, we tend to assume that no form of Christian monasticism existed other than that known to the West from Egypt.[23]

But, as we have seen, this was far from the case. If we look out at the great third world of Christianity in Africa and the Middle East, we find a set of widely diverging social and religious landscapes, each characterized by very different views as to whether a monk should or should not work. The Egyptian model was not the only option. We need to appreciate the power and the sheer geographical extent of the alternative model represented by the Manichees and by the "angelic" monks of Syria. For, when seen against the spacious background of Eurasia as a whole, the Manichees and the monks of Syria were the norm, and the self-supporting communities of Egypt and the West were the exception. Indeed, it is quite possible to imagine the emergence of a Christian monasticism that closely resembled the position of the *sangha* in Buddhist countries—communities of ascetic virtuosi fed by their laity as part of an unceasing spiritual exchange by which base matter (in the form of food, clothing, and shelter) was offered in return for the ethereal, spiritual goods of prayer and preaching.[24]

Yet this did not happen. The "Buddhist way" was blocked by a tenacious alternative. Hence the excitement of the clash of ideas that pitted one form of Christian monasticism against the other across the Fertile Crescent, as Egypt diverged from Syria. By following this divergence we are listening in to the western end of a debate on wealth, labor, and the monks that was as wide as Asia itself. An entire spectrum of views on the nature of society and on the role of labor in defining the human person was at stake in every region and in every religious group, Buddhist, Manichaean, or Christian.

Seen from the viewpoint of Asia as a whole, the significance of this debate was that it was inconclusive. Parts of Byzantium, parts of the Christian Middle East (especially Egypt), and all of western Europe did not follow a pattern of monastic life that was normal throughout Asia east of the Pamirs—in northern India, Central Asia, and western China.

It is a telling juxtaposition. In the fourth century, the great Chinese Buddhist pilgrim Faxian (Fa Hsien) walked all the way from China to northern India following the route of the Buddhist *sangha*, along a chain of monasteries. Each one of these monasteries was totally supported by the alms of the laity. Faxian spoke of the Buddhist regions through which he had passed as "Lands of the Begging Bowl."[25] Seen from China, Europe and Byzantium stood out as exceptions. Only those remote and peripheral territories failed to become what most of Asia had become. They did not become "Lands of the Begging Bowl."

Nor should we underestimate the consequences of the predominance, in much of Byzantine Christianity and in all the Latin West, of the imaginative model of society implied by the stubborn Egyptian emphasis on the labor of the monks.

Put in a nutshell, human society, and the human suffering associated with real divisions between rich and poor, took on a density that was lacking in the "cosmic" option of the Manichees and even (for all the deep compassion and sharp disgust for the lust for power and land that characterized contemporary society which appear in the lives of many Syrian saints and in the *Book of Steps*) in the "angelic" option of the holy men of Syria.

For both of these—Manichees and Syrians—human society had somehow lacked substance. Dwarfed by the majesty of a fallen cosmos, as with the Manichees, or overshadowed by the great sadness of Adam's fall into a world of labor, as with the monks of Syria, the present-day organization of society itself, and its all-too-palpable divisions between rich and poor, represented only a thin sliver of the human condition. The division of rich and poor seemed insubstantial compared with the stark division between the freedom of a spirit-filled few and the dull servitude to material things in which the majority of humanity, rich and poor alike, found itself caught.

Writings in this tradition faced normal society with an almost disturbing serenity, which resembled that of the great third-century pagan sage Plotinus when he argued against the Christians. He claimed that Christians were unduly concerned with issues of wealth and poverty. Plotinus, however, viewed society from a great height: "But if anyone objects to wealth and poverty and the fact that all have not an equal share in things of this kind, . . . he is ignorant that the good and wise man does not look for equality in these things . . . he leaves concern of this kind to others. He has learned that there are only two kinds of life here below, one for the good and wise and one for the mass of men."[26]

By contrast, in claiming to live from the labor of their hands, the monks of Egypt asserted (in the heavy language of work and food) that they were not above the "mass of men." They were not "angels." Rather, they were fully paid up human members of a human society characterized by sharp contours. These contours were drawn, in the most blatant manner possible, by differences of access to food. Food could only be acquired by work. Condemned to work so as to eat, the monks were linked by labor to the sufferings of the poor. They were held responsible, along with laypersons, for alleviating the all-too-real ills of society through real labor for the real distribution of alms to the real poor.

The monks of Egypt (like other monks from other Christian regions) have all too easily been dismissed, as by the majestic Edward Gibbon, as "those unhappy exiles from social life."[27] But it is often those who take a stance outside society who think most clearly about its ills, and who can bring its tensions to the surface in dramatic and arresting gestures. This is what happened between Syria and Egypt in the fourth and fifth centuries. It happened in two significantly different ways. In Syria, the monks revived the great myths of primal leisure, and, in so doing, problematized a society caught in the dull creak of toil. By contrast, by insisting on the necessity of manual labor and on the duty of the monk to work so as to support the real poor, the monks of Egypt brought a grittier flavor to the social imagination of their age. They contributed, in their own way, to an imaginative victory which, ever since that time, has placed at the very heart of our modern conscience a model of society divided between rich and poor, in which the rich have a religious and a moral duty to support the poor.

So let me end, in Egypt, with the little known words of the great Coptic monastic prayer to the Archangel Michael: "We find the intercession of Michael in the strenuous work of our hands . . . in the quietness of the oxen and the growth of the lambs . . . in the body of the vine and the gladness which is in the wine . . . in the fatness and the savor of the olives. . . . And we find the intercession of Michael [also] when he is gentle towards those who are weary with toil and when he gives them strength."[28]

Notes

Introduction

1. Brown, *Poverty and Leadership in the Later Roman Empire*; and *Through the Eye of a Needle.*
2. Silber, *Virtuosity, Charisma and Social Order.*
3. Holman, *The Hungry Are Dying;* Finn, *Almsgiving in the Later Roman Empire;* Freu, *Les figures du pauvre dans les sources italiennes.*
4. Brown, *The Ransom of the Soul.*
5. Gibbon, *Decline and Fall of the Roman Empire*, chap. 38: "General Observations on the Fall of the Roman Empire in the West," 2:439.
6. Bowersock, "Old and New Rome in the Late Antique Near East."
7. Millar, *A Greek Roman Empire.*
8. A team directed by Professor David Michelson of Vanderbilt University is now rendering accessible the abundant literature of the Syriac world, along with a complete gazetteer of its literary centers in late antiquity and in the Middle Ages. See Syriaca.org.
9. Bowersock, *Hellenism in Late Antiquity.*
10. Török, *Transfigurations of Hellenism.*

1 "Treasure in Heaven" and "The Poor among the Saints"

1. Brown, *Through the Eye of a Needle.*
2. Jerusalem Talmud, *Peah* 11.15b, 63–75, trans. Schwab, 2:7; trans. Wewers, 2:2, pp. 10–11.
3. *Porphyrius "Gegen die Christen,"* 82–83, fragment no. 58; taken from Macarius of Magnesia, *Monogenes* 3.5, ed. Goulet, 80–81.
4. Julian, Letter 40, ed. Wright, 3:126.
5. Koch, "Der Schatz im Himmel," 52.
6. Urbach, "Treasure Above," 118, 124.
7. Luomanen, "Where Did Another Rich Man Come From?"
8. Brown, *Through the Eye of a Needle*, 83–86; and "Treasure in Heaven."
9. Anderson, *Charity*, 7–8.
10. Theissen, *The Social Setting of Pauline Christianity;* Meeks, *The First Urban Christians.*

11. Megitt, *Paul, Poverty and Survival;* Friesen, "Poverty in Pauline Studies."

12. See esp. Osiek, *Rich and Poor in the Shepherd of Hermas.*

13. Hermas, *The Shepherd,* Similitude 2.52, ed. Joly, 214–18.

14. Babylonian Talmud, Ḥullin 92a, trans. E. Cashdan (1948), 516.

15. Georgi, *Remembering the Poor,* 141.

16. Downs, *The Offering of the Gentiles.*

17. Macarius of Magnesia, *Monogénès* 3.32, ed. Goulet, 192; *Porphyrius "Gegen die Christen,"* ed. Harnack, fragment no. 58, p. 58.

18. Buell, "'Be Not One Who Stretches Out Hands,'" 42.

19. *Didache* 1.6, *La Doctrine des Douze Apôtres = Didachè,* ed. Rordorf and Tuilier, 146. See Niederwimmer, *The Didache,* 83–86.

20. *Didache* 11.5 and 9, ed. Rordorf and Tuilier, 184–86; Niederwimmer, *Didache,* 175–77.

21. Barclay, "Money and Meetings," 120.

22. Schöllgen, *Die Anfänge der Professionalisierung,* 21–25. See now esp. Gordon, "Individuality, Selfhood and Power in the Second Century," 165–66.

23. For this aspect of *ponos,* see esp. Finley, *The Ancient Economy,* 41–44; and Schiavone, *The End of the Past,* 37, on work "as a kind of dead zone for civilization . . . a 'dark hole' in community life."

24. Austin and Vidal-Naquet, *Economic and Social History of Ancient Greece,* 16.

25. See Wischmeyer, *Die Kultur des Buches Jesus Sirach,* 64–65, 259–365.

26. Gregory of Nyssa, *Contra Eunomium* 1.49, *Patrologia Graeca* 45:264B.

27. Vaggione, *Eunomius of Cyzicus and the Nicene Revolution,* 1–11, tells a very different story from that told by Gregory.

28. Hamel, *Poverty and Charity in Roman Palestine,* 134–36.

29. Eusebius, *Ecclesiastical History* 3.20.1–3.

30. William Shakespeare, *Midsummer Night's Dream,* act 5, scene 2.

31. Gordon, "Monotheism, Henotheism, Megatheism," 673.

2 "Do It through the Bishop"

1. Origen, *Contra Celsum* 1.28, trans. Chadwick, 28.

2. Lucian, *The Passing of Peregrinus* 11–13, ed. Harmon, 5:12–14. See now König, "The Cynic and Christian Lives of Lucian's Peregrinus," 229–31; Spickermann, "Philosophical Standards and Intellectual Life-Style."

3. See now Pietzner, *Bildung, Elite und Konkurrenz.*

4. Artemidorus, *Oneirocriticon* 3.53.

5. Dio Chrysostom, *Euboikos* 7.81–93; see Brunt, "Aspects of the Social Thought of Dio Chrysostom," 9. Travelers seem always to have a weak spot for the apparent utopias of obligation-free giving which they encounter. Christopher Columbus described the Caribs who surrounded his first settlement at Navidad as "a people of love without venality": see Fleming, "Columbus as a Scriptural Exegete."

6. Schwartz, *Were the Jews a Mediterranean Society?*, 174.
7. Schwartz, *Were the Jews a Mediterranean Society?*, 18.
8. Babylonian Talmud, *Sanhedrin* 52ab, cited in Kalmin, *The Sage in Jewish Society in Late Antiquity*, 32.
9. *Didascalia Apostolorum*, ed. Stewart-Sykes, 65–66.
10. Schöllgen, *Die Anfänge der Professionalisierung*, 2.
11. *Didascalia Apostolorum* 15.7 [3.10], ed. Stewart-Sykes, 190.
12. *Didascalia Apostolorum* 10.2 [2.35], ed. Stewart-Sykes, 158.
13. *Didascalia Apostolorum* 10.5 [2.36], ed. Stewart-Sykes, 158.
14. Schöllgen, *Die Anfänge der Professionalisierung*, 114–34.
15. Eusebius, *Ecclesiastical History* 6.43.11.
16. Schöllgen, *Die Anfänge der Professionalisierung*, 100.
17. Duncan-Jones, *The Economy of the Roman Empire*, 277–83.
18. Brown, *Poverty and Leadership in the Later Roman Empire*, 24–26; and *Through the Eye of a Needle*, 42–43.
19. Cyprian, Letter 62, ed. Hartel, 698–701; trans. Clarke, *The Letters of Saint Cyprian*, 3:95–97.
20. Cyprian, Letter 62.5, ed. Hartel, 701, trans. Clarke, 3:97.
21. Cyprian, *De operibus et elemosynis* 7, ed. Hartel, 1:379.
22. *Didascalia Apostolorum* 9.4.5 [2.58], ed. Stewart-Sykes, 152–53. Cyprian, Letters 1.1.2, trans. Clarke, 1:58; and 39.5.2, trans. Clarke, 2:154–57. Schöllgen, "*Sportulae*."
23. Nijf, *The Civic World of Professional Associations*, 119.
24. Lendon, *Empire of Honor*, 100–101.
25. Origen, *In Numeros* 22; see Schöllgen, *Die Anfänge der Professionalisierung*, 12.
26. Optatus of Milevis, *De schismate Donatistarum* 1.17, trans. Edwards, *Against the Donatists*, 17.
27. Potter, *Constantine the Emperor*, 193; see, in general, the outstanding study of Shaw, *Sacred Violence*.
28. Optatus, *De schismate Donatistarum*, trans. Edwards, Appendix 1: *Gesta apud Zenophilum*, 154; see also Duval, *Chrétiens d'Afrique*, 169–73, 408–20.
29. North's "The Development of Religious Pluralism" remains the classic statement of this view. See now the incisive remarks of Gordon, "Monotheism, Henotheism, Megatheism."
30. Price, "Religious Mobility in the Roman Empire," presents but questions this view in a masterly posthumously published article.
31. Hopkins, "Christian Number and Its Implications." This is a trenchant contribution to the discussion, in the same volume of the *Journal of Early Christian Studies*, of the ambitious but disappointing study of R. Stark, *The Rise of Christianity: A Sociologist Reconsiders History* (Princeton: Princeton University Press, 1996).
32. Dodds, *Pagans and Christians in an Age of Anxiety*.

33. Carrié and Rousselle, *L'empire romain*, 433–38.
34. Cameron, *Christianity and the Rhetoric of Empire*, 32–39; Pietzner, *Bildung, Elite und Konkurrenz*, 168–203.
35. Alexander of Lycopolis, *Contra Manichaei opiniones* 16, trans. Horst and Mansfeld, 88.
36. This issue is central in modern discussions of the nature of the Pauline communities: see Longenecker, "Exposing the Economic Middle."
37. Scheidel, "Stratification, Deprivation," 54.
38. Beck, "Ritual, Myth."
39. Beck, "Ritual, Myth," 176.
40. Beck, "Ritual, Myth," 178.
41. Beck, "Ritual, Myth," 153–58, 175.
42. Luijendijk, *"Greetings in the Lord,"* 116.
43. Grafton and Williams, *Christianity and the Transformation of the Book*, 131.
44. Eusebius, *Ecclesiastical History* 6.23.
45. Markschies, *Kaiserzeitliche christliche Theologie*, 107. See now Pietzner, *Bildung, Elite und Konkurrenz*, 273–339.
46. On the problem of libraries and patronage in general in the third and fourth centuries, see Brown, *Through the Eye of a Needle*, 275–79.
47. Daley, *The Hope of the Early Church*, 2nd ed., 59.
48. Ulrich, "What Do We Know about Justin's 'School'?," esp. 69.
49. Rives, "Christian Expansion and Christian Ideology," 32–38.
50. Zanker, *The Mask of Socrates*, 304, 293.
51. Judge, "The Earliest Use of Monachos"; Morard, "Monachos, Moine"; Wipszycka, "Quand a-t-on commencé à voir?"; Bumazhnov, *"Monakhos esti."*
52. Rubenson, "Monasticism and the Philosophical Heritage."
53. Funk, "The Reconstruction of the Manichaean *Kephalaia*"; Pettipiece, *Pentadic Redaction of the Manichaean Kephalaia*.

3 "The Treasuries That Are in the Heights"

1. Schwartz, *Were the Jews a Mediterranean Society?*, 27.
2. *Acts of Judas Thomas* 85.
3. Lucian, *Demonax* 63, ed. and trans. Harmon, 1:170.
4. *Didascalia Apostolorum* 19 [5.1], ed. Stewart-Sykes, 202.
5. Sahner, *Among the Ruins*, 6.
6. West, *The East Face of Helicon*, 4.
7. Ward-Perkins, "Frontiere politiche e frontiere cullturali," 395 (page nos. are to the English summary).
8. Ps.-Clement, *Ad Virgines* 2.6, *Patrologia Graeca* 1:433A.
9. *Bulletin de Correspondance Hellénique* 21 (1897): 60–61.
10. Gardner, "Some Comments on Mani."
11. Smith, "Dendrites and Other Standers." See also Bailey and Mabbett, *The Sociology of Early Buddhism*, 86.

12. Kretschmar, "Ein Beitrag zur Frage"; Theissen, *Sociology of Early Palestinian Christianity*, 24–30.

13. Tardieu, "La diffusion du bouddhisme"; and *Manichaeism*, 52–53; Lieu, *Manichaeism in the Later Roman Empire*. See now Vaissière, "Mani en Chine au vie siècle." See also Lim, "Unity and Diversity among the Western Manichaeans."

14. *Psalms of Heracleides*, in Allberry, *A Manichaean Psalmbook*, part 2, 195: 8–12; see now Richter, *Die Heracleides-Psalmen* 5:56–61, pp. 80–81.

15. Tardieu, *Manichaeism*, 21–24; Brian-Baker, *Manichaeism*, 22–29, 70–77; Crone, *The Nativist Prophets of Early Islamic Iran*, 194–96, 306–13.

16. Brown, "The Diffusion of Manichaeism"; Gardner and Lieu, "From Narmouthis (Medinat Madi) to Kellis (Ismant al-Kharab)." Much of this material has been translated in Gardner and Lieu, *Manichaean Texts*.

17. I. Gardner, *Papyri Kellis Coptici* 32.1–13, in *Coptic Documentary Texts from Kellis*, 79.

18. Baker-Brian, *Manichaeism*, 54.

19. *Papyri Kellis Coptici* 32.1–13, *Coptic Documentary Texts*, 214; trans. Gardner and Lieu, *Manichaean Texts*, 277 (my emphasis).

20. *Papyri Kellis Coptici* 32.13, *Coptic Documentary Texts*, 214; trans. Gardner and Lieu, *Manichaean Texts*, 277; see Gardner, "'With a Pure Heart and a Truthful Tongue,'" 81, where the Sun and Moon are "the visible presence of God in this world."

21. *Papyri Kellis Coptici* 31.17–23, *Coptic Documentary Texts*, 210; trans. Gardner and Lieu, *Manichaean Texts*, 277–78.

22. Brown, "Alms and the Afterlife."

23. Augustine, *Confessions* 4.1.1. See BeDuhn, *Augustine's Manichaean Dilemma* 1, 42–69; Brown, *Through the Eye of a Needle*, 157–60.

24. Edited in BeDuhn and Harrison, "The Tebessa Codex"; and Stein, *Manichaica Latina* 3:1; trans. Gardner and Lieu, *Manichaean Texts*, 268.

25. Baker-Brian, *Manichaeism*, 62.

26. Augustine, *De moribus manichaeorum* 15.36, trans. Gardner and Lieu, *Manichaean Texts*, 246.

27. BeDuhn, *The Manichaean Body*, 163–208.

28. See esp. the debate with the Marcionites in Irenaeus, *Adversus Haereses* 4.30.3, ed. Rousseau, 782—the goods of this world are not "alien" to God and so can be used and offered by Christians.

29. *Apostolic Constitutions* 8.40, ed. Metzger, 224.

30. Rajak, "The 'Gifts of God' at Sardis"; Luijendijk, "*Greetings in the Lord*," 126, on *P. Oxy.* 12.1492.

31. Augustine, *De haeresibus* 46.11, trans. Gardner and Lieu, *Manichaean Texts*, 189.

32. Chavannes and Pelliot, "Un traité manichéen retrouvé en Chine."

33. BeDuhn, "The Metabolism of Salvation"; Baker-Brian, *Manichaeism*, 120–31.

34. Černý, *Coptic Etymological Dictionary*, 94.
35. Augustine, *Enarrationes in Psalmos* 140.12; *P. Rylands Greek* 469.12–14; trans. Gardner and Lieu, *Manichaean Texts*, 115; see also Cyril of Jerusalem, *Catecheses* 6.32.
36. Augustine, *De moribus manichaeorum* 2.3.20–18.66.
37. *The Cologne Mani Codex: Concerning the Origin of His Body*, 97.1–99.1, p. 78; Augustine, *Enarrationes in Psalmos* 140.12, trans. Gardner and Lieu, *Manichaean Texts*, 245.
38. Mani, *Kephalaion* 150, p. 365, lines 11–17.
39. Bagnall, *The Kellis Agricultural Account Books*.
40. *Cologne Mani Codex*, 9.1, p. 12.

4 "In the Likeness of the Angels"

1. Alster, *Proverbs of Ancient Sumer*, 343.
2. *Atrahasis*, trans. Foster, *Before the Muses*, 159–66.
3. Genesis 3:17–19.
4. Hesiod, *Works and Days*, 286–91; West, *The East Face of Helicon*, 276–333; Gatz, *Goldene Zeit und sinnverwandte Vorstellungen*.
5. *Atrahasis* 190, trans. Foster, 165.
6. Cauvin, *The Birth of the Gods*, 67–72.
7. Escolan, *Monachisme et Église*.
8. Caner, *Wandering, Begging Monks*.
9. From an extensive literature, I have gained most from Nedungatt, "The Covenanters of the Early Syriac-Speaking Church"; Murray, "The Exhortation to Candidates for Ascetical Vows"; Brock, "Early Syrian Asceticism"; Griffith, "Images of Ephraem."
10. Shils, *Center and Periphery*, 251.
11. Nedungatt, "The Covenanters," 203.
12. Escolan, *Monachisme et Église*, 51.
13. Murray, "Exhortation to Candidates," 59; Griffith, "Images of Ephraem," 10, 12.
14. Burkitt, *Early Christianity outside the Roman Empire*, 139.
15. Brock, "Early Syrian Asceticism," 5.
16. Nedungatt, "The Covenanters," 444, likens them to modern lay institutes. Singing, however, was not mere music. It was treated as a palpable expression of the presence of the Holy Spirit in the church. See Brown, *The Body and Society*, 101–2.
17. Skoyles, *Aphrahat the Persian Sage*, 85.
18. Ephraem, *Hymns on the Epiphany* 8, cited by Murray, "Exhortation to Candidates," 65.
19. Escolan, *Monachisme et Église*, 154, 181; see Brown, *The Rise of Western Christendom*, 414–19.
20. Escolan, *Monachisme et Église*, 198.

21. *Liber Graduum*, ed. M. Kmoskó, trans. Kitchen and Parmentier, *The Book of Steps*. Kmoskó's text is reprinted with a facing translation by Kitchen and Parmentier in *The Syriac Book of Steps* (Gorgias Press). For the sake of convenience, I shall cite the column numbers of Kmoskó, under the title of *Liber Graduum*. These column numbers are inserted in both the translation and the reprint of Kitchen and Parmentier.

22. Heal and Kitchen, *Breaking the Mind*. I am greatly indebted to Kyle Smith for having brought this volume to my attention soon after this chapter was written.

23. On the context, see now Smith, "A Last Disciple of the Apostles."

24. Stewart, "By Way of a Preface," xi. On the Messalians, see esp. Stewart, *"Working the Earth of the Heart"*; and Fitschen, *Messalianismus und Anti-messalianismus*, 108–28.

25. Scully, "Lowering in Order to be Raised," 297.

26. *Liber Graduum* 14.2, Kmoskó 328, trans. 136; 25.2, Kmoskó 739, trans. 239; 25.8, Kmoskó 752, trans. 298; 26.2, Kmoskó 760, 302.

27. See now Kofsky and Ruzer, "Reading the Ascetic Ideal."

28. *Liber Graduum* 25.2, Kmoskó 736, trans. 292. Certain rabbis also argued that Adam did not work in the garden of Eden. His "work" consisted in studying Torah: Diamond, *Holy Men and Hunger Artists*, 23–33.

29. *Liber Graduum* 15.2, Kmoskó 339, trans. 100.

30. *Liber Graduum* 20.6, Kmoskó 543, trans. 216.

31. *Liber Graduum* 20.6, Kmoskó 543, trans. 216.

32. See esp. Juhl, *Die Askese im Liber Graduum*, 71–76.

33. *Liber Graduum* 15.9, Kmoskó 356, trans. 146.

34. Harvey, "The Sense of a Stylite."

35. *Liber Graduum* 15.4, Kmoskó 343, trans. 142; see also Cramer, *Die Engelvorstellungen bei Ephräm dem Syrer*.

36. Rabbi Abbahu in Levene, *The Early Syrian Fathers*, 127.

37. *Syriac Life of Symeon* 98, trans. Doran, *The Lives of Simeon Stylites*, 171–72.

38. Theodoret of Cyrrhus, *Historia religiosa* 26.22, trans. Price, *A History of the Monks of Syria*, 170.

39. *Liber Graduum* 22.6, Kmoskó 647, trans. 257. See Westerhoff, *Das Paulusverständnis im Liber Graduum*, 174–82.

40. *Liber Graduum* 9.6, Kmoskó 216, trans. 92–93; and 22.7, Kmoskó 649, trans. 257.

41. *Liber Graduum* 22.7, Kmoskó 649, trans. 257.

42. Decker, *"Tilling the Hateful Earth,"* 250.

43. Sarris, *Economy and Society*, 122.

44. Decker, *"Tilling the Hateful Earth,"* 193.

45. Decker, *"Tilling the Hateful Earth,"* 44, 66–79.

46. Decker, *"Tilling the Hateful Earth,"* 196, on the Negev.

47. L. Robert, *Hellenica* 11–12 (1960): 321–25.

48. Robert, *Hellenica* 11–12, 325.
49. Sarris, *Economy and Society*, 125; Decker, *"Tilling the Hateful Earth,"* 52. On granaries, hoarding, and wealth, see Brown, *Through the Eye of a Needle*, 14.
50. Butler, *Publications of the Princeton University Archaeological Expedition, Greek and Latin Inscriptions*, 98, no. 1023.
51. Butler, *Publications of the Princeton University Archaeological Expedition, Greek and Latin Inscriptions*, 86–99, nos. 1005–24.
52. *Codex Theodosianus* 12.1.63. See now Lenski, "Valens and the Monks."
53. Libanius, *Oratio* 30.48, ed. Förster, 3:114; trans. Norman, 144.
54. Burghart, "Renunciation in the Religious Traditions," 641.
55. Augustine, *Retractationes* 2.21.
56. Loraux, *"Ponos."* See also Desmond, *The Greek Praise of Poverty*, 27–103.
57. Loraux, *"Ponos,"* 176; see Robert, *Hellenica* 11–12, 347, for its wide usage in epigraphy.
58. James, *The Will to Believe*, 214; see Slater, *William James on Ethics and Faith*.
59. Libanius, *Oratio* 4.15–17, ed. Förster, 1:292. See esp. Doukellis, *Libanios et la terre*, 151.
60. Daloz, *Le travail*, 64.
61. Harl, "La prise de conscience"; M.-D. Chenu, *La théologie au douzième siècle*, 44–51, trans. Taylor and Little, 37–48.
62. Sarris, *Economy and Society*, 117.
63. Sarris, *Economy and Society*, 120.
64. Libanius, *Oratio* 11.26, ed. Förster, 1:445; see Doukellis, *Libanios et la terre*, 190.
65. Sarris, *Economy and Society*, 117–18; Banaji, "Aristocracies, Peasantries."
66. Theodoret, *Historia religiosa* 14.4, trans. Price, 111–12.
67. *Syriac Life of Symeon* 131, trans. Doran, 196.
68. *Life of Alexander Akoimêtos* 33, trans. Caner, *Wandering, Begging Monks*, 269.
69. John of Ephesus, *Lives of the Eastern Saints: 1 Life of Habib, Patrologia Orientalis* 17:8.
70. Ephraem, *On the Crucifixion* 8.1.3–6; see Kronholm, *Motifs from Genesis I–II*, 124.
71. Theodoret, *Historia religiosa* 8.15, trans. Price, 79. See Brown, "The Rise and Function of the Holy Man," 120–30.
72. Theodoret, *Historia religiosa* 9.14, trans. Price, 87.
73. Theodoret, *Historia religiosa* 9.15, trans. Price, 87.
74. Theodoret, *Historia religiosa* 9.4, trans. Price, 83.
75. Theodoret, *Historia religiosa* 13.3, trans. Price, 101.
76. Escolan, *Monachisme et Église*, 182–225.

5 "The Work of the Hands . . . an Ornament to the Men of Egypt"

1. Julian, *Oratio* 7, 224B, ed. Wright, 2:122.
2. Judge, "The Earliest Use of Monachos"; Wipszycka, "*Anachôrités, erémités,*" 161–65; and now *Moines et communautés monastiques,* 308–16.
3. Thonemann, "Amphilochius of Iconium," esp. 190, 195.
4. Zosimus, *Historia nova* 5.23, trans. Ridley, 111.
5. BeDuhn, *The Manichaean Body,* 202.
6. *Papyri Kellis Coptici* 51.06–8, in Gardner, *Kellis Literary Texts,* 54.
7. *Syriac Life of Symeon* 42, trans. Doran, 126.
8. López, *Shenoute of Atripe,* 8.
9. *Pap. Turner* 54, in *Papyri Greek and Egyptian,* 198–203.
10. Athanasius, *Life of Anthony* 2.3, ed. Bartelink, 132; trans. Vivian and Athanassakis, 56–59.
11. Wipszycka, *Moines et communautés monastiques,* 259–60.
12. Athanasius, *Life of Anthony* 2.5, ed. Bartelink, 134; trans. Vivian and Athanassakis, 58–59.
13. Athanasius, *Life of Anthony* 3.6, ed. Bartelink, 138; trans. Vivian and Athanassakis, 62–63.
14. Goehring, "The Encroaching Desert," 281 (the phrase occurs in the abstract of the article).
15. See esp. Brakke, *Athanasius and the Politics of Asceticism,* 201–65.
16. Chaîne, "La double recension," 241 (trans. 261, my emphasis).
17. Epiphanius of Salamis, *Panarion* 80.4, *Patrologia Graeca* 42:762D.
18. Jerome, Letter 22:34–36. See Vogüé, *Histoire littéraire du movement monastique,* 292–314; and Caseau, "L'image du mauvais moine."
19. Augustine, *De moribus ecclesiae catholicae* 1.33.70.
20. Augustine, *De moribus ecclesiae catholicae* 1.32.67.
21. Rufinus, *Historia monachorum* 18.3, ed. Schulz-Flügel, 350; the Greek is edited by A. J. Festugière, *Historia monachorum in Aegypto,* 115.
22. Augustine, *De opere monachorum* 13.14–14.15.
23. Brown, *Augustine of Hippo,* 144.
24. Williams, *Authorized Lives in Early Christian Biography,* 111. See also Johnson, *The Life and Miracles of Thekla,* 104–9; Heiser, *Die Paulusinszenierung des Johannes Chrysostomus.* It is the same with the "biographical" treatments of the Patriarchs in the sermons of Ambrose: see now Rousseau, "Homily and Exegesis in the Patristic Age," 22: "we need to know enough about him to *imitate* the man."
25. Shenoute of Atripe, Letter 30, ed. Leipoldt and Crum, 93.7.
26. *Apophthegmata Patrum,* John Colobos 2, *Patrologia Graeca* 65:203D–204A; *The Sayings of the Desert Fathers,* trans. Ward, 73.
27. Bagnall, *Egypt in Late Antiquity,* 8.
28. Wipszycka, *Moines et communautés monastiques,* 116.
29. Wipszycka, "The Nag Hammadi Library and the Monks," 189.

30. Wipszycka, *Moines et communautés monastiques*, 227.

31. Elm, introduction to "Charisma and Society," 349.

32. Leyser, "The Uses of the Desert," 119.

33. *Bohairic Life of Pachomius* 185, trans. Veilleux, *Pachomian Koinonia* 1:223–24.

34. *Apophthegmata Patrum*, Serapion 2: 416C.

35. Brown, *The Body and Society*, 235–37.

36. *Apophthegmata Patrum*, Poemen 22: 328AB.

37. For a magnificent evocation of the meaning of the harvest in the ancient world, see now Shaw, *Bringing in the Sheaves*, 73–88. Monks could be mistreated like any other laborers. See Theodore, *Instructions* 14, in Pachomius, trans. Veilleux, *Pachomian Koinonia* 3:101: "let us toil away at the work to which we have been sent, even if we are struck, insulted, imprisoned, even if we come back to the monastery spattered with blood from the blows." But they were often paid special wages as a form of covert alms: Rufinus, *Historia monachorum* 18.3, Schulz-Flügel, 350; Festugière, 114; see Wipszycka, *Moines et communautés monastiques*, 488.

38. *Apophthegmata Patrum*, Isaiah 5: 181BC.

39. *Apophthegmata Patrum*, Isaac 4: 225A. So "dispossessed" was Isaac that he did not realize that it was his own former field that he was harvesting. Does this mean that he was still paid rent by a tenant? The anecdote is a warning that the story was told so as to encourage a general mental detachment. It need not assume a total renunciation of property.

40. I owe much to Lukas A. Schachner, "Economic Production in the Monasteries," 199.

41. Schachner, "Economic Production in the Monasteries," 220.

42. *Apophthegmata Patrum*, Megethius 1: 300D.

43. Wipszycka, *Moines et communautés monastiques*, 485. This judgment may have to be nuanced in the light of Schachner, "Economic Production in the Monasteries," 199–202, 218.

44. Palladius, *Historia Lausiaca* 10.6, ed. Bartelink, 48; trans. Meyer, 45.

45. The concern led to exemplary tales of price-fixing to avoid bargaining: Pachomius, *Paralipomena* 23, trans. Veilleux, *Pachomian Koinonia* 3:47. We need not believe them: see Wipszycka, *Moines et communautés monastiques*, 532. For a ruling on bargaining, see *Apophthegmata Patrum*, Pistamon: 376AB; for the favorite monk of a well-to-do family, known from his stand at the marketplace: *Apophthegmata Patrum*, Daniel 3: 153C.

46. *Apophthegmata Patrum*, Lucius 1: 259B. Out of sixteen coins, Lucius assigned two to the poor. The rigorous monastic ideal of *sufficientia* could lead to radical criticisms of wealth: see Brown, *Through the Eye of a Needle*, 315–16.

47. Bagnall, "Monks and Property"; Choat, "Property Ownership and Tax Payment."

48. Laniado, "The Early Byzantine State."

49. Wipszycka, *"Anachôrités, erémités,"* 168; and *Moines et communautés monastiques*, 315–16.
50. Bagnall, *Egypt in Late Antiquity*, 296–97.
51. See, e.g., Rubenson, *The Letters of Saint Anthony*. This has been sharply criticized by Gould, "Recent Work on Monastic Origins," 411, on the grounds that Rubenson's view unduly "gentrifies" the monks.
52. Bagnall, *Egypt in Late Antiquity*, 303.
53. Schopen, *Buddhist Monks and Business Matters*.
54. Turner, *Truthfulness, Realism, Historicity*, 4.
55. John Cassian, *Institutiones cénobitiques* 4.22, ed. Guy, 150–52.

6 "You Are a Human Being . . . You Must Work . . . in Order to Eat"

1. Brown, "The Rise and Function of the Holy Man," 110–12.
2. Goehring, "The World Engaged," 40; Brown, *Body and Society*, 243–47.
3. Amélineau, *Monuments pour servir à l'histoire*, civ.
4. Wipszycka, "The Institutional Church," points to this lacuna.
5. Giorda, *Il regno di Dio in terra*, 43–67; and *Monachesimo e istituzioni ecclesiastiche in Egitto*, 19.
6. *P. Lond.* VI.1926, in Bell, *Jews and Christians in Egypt*, 109, and also translated in Bagnall, *Egypt in Late Antiquity*, 299–300.
7. Minnen, "Saving History?," 64, 89.
8. Papaconstantinou, *Le culte des saints en Égypte*. For an excellent recent study of oracle books, many of which were connected to the shrines of martyrs, see now Luijendijk, *Forbidden Oracles?*, 49–51.
9. *Archiv des Nepheros*, ed. Kramer and Shelton, 7.
10. *Archiv des Nepheros*, no. 4.30, pp. 45, 47.
11. *Archiv des Nepheros*, no. 3.8, p. 43; no. 10.10, p. 67.
12. *Archiv des Nepheros*, no. 15.3, p. 81.
13. *Archiv des Nepheros*, no. 5.14, p. 49.
14. Minnen, "Saving History?," 89.
15. Decker, *"Tilling the Hateful Earth,"* 229.
16. Lutz, *Musonius Rufus*, 82.
17. Babylonian Talmud, *Shabbat* 116c, trans. H. Freedman (1938), 2:571. See Krauss, *Griechische und lateinische Lehnwörter*, 2:446–47; and Brown, *Power and Persuasion*, 63–64.
18. Wipszycka is particularly insistent on this point. The handicrafts privileged in monastic texts could not have brought in much: basketry was too widespread as a domestic industry for a profitable market to emerge. See esp. "Le monachisme égyptien et les villes," 135; "Les aspects économiques"; "Contribution à l'étude de l'économie"; "Les formes institutionnelles," 149–50; and *Moines et communautés monastiques*, 218. But see Schachner, "Economic Production in the Monasteries," 199–202, for a slightly higher valuation of basketwork and evidence for monastic spe-

cialization for a market. On any account, monastic income still needed supplementing from other sources not mentioned in the literature—primarily from agriculture, but also from weaving: see Schachner, 252–66.

19. *Apophthegmata Patrum*, Serinos 2: 417B.
20. *Apophthegmata Patrum*, John Kolobos 40: 217BC.
21. Palladius, *Historia Lausiaca* 10.3, ed. Bartelink, 46; trans. Meyer, 44–45.
22. Palladius, *Historia Lausiaca* 18.27, ed. Bartelink, 94.
23. *Apophthegmata Patrum*, John Kolobos 2: 204A.
24. Synesius, *Dion* 7.4, ed. Terzaghi, 2:251–52; trans. Fitzgerald, 1:161. See Brown, *Power and Persuasion in Late Antiquity*, 115–17, 136–39.
25. S.v. "Arbeit," *Lexikon der Ägyptologie* (Wiesbaden: O. Harrassowitz, 1975), 1:370.
26. Shaw, *Bringing in the Sheaves*, fig. 4.5 on p. 162.
27. Vandier, *La famine dans l'Égypte*.
28. Vandier, *La famine dans l'Égypte*, 45–48.
29. Horden and Purcell, *The Corrupting Sea*, 186–90. Cf. Will, *Bureaucracy and Famine in Eighteenth-Century China*.
30. Vandier, *La famine dans l'Égypte*, 48–51.
31. Assmann, *Death and Salvation*, 304.
32. Assmann, *Death and Salvation*, 139.
33. Černý, *Coptic Etymological Dictionary*, 277; Vandier, *La famine dans l'Égypte*, 93–97.
34. *Bohairic Life of Pachomius* 100, trans. Veilleux, *Pachomian Koinonia* 1: 137–38.
35. Frank, *The Memory of the Eyes*, 49–61. By contrast, Wipszycka, *Moines et communautés monastiques*, 13, 404, does not consider the account to be entirely fictional. See now Williams, *Authorized Lives*, 137–42.
36. Fentress and Wickham, *Social Memory*, 74.
37. Rufinus, *Historia monachorum* 10.29.188, Festugière, 87; Schulz-Flügel, 320.
38. *Historia monachorum* 12.16.93, Festugière, 97; Schulz-Flügel, 331.
39. *Historia monachorum* 10.24.157, Festugière, 85; Schulz-Flügel, 318.
40. *Historia monachorum* 8.23.153, Festugière, 55–56; Schulz-Flügel, 293. Schulz-Flügel finds no parallel to this belief (15n39).
41. Moschos, *Eschatologie im ägyptischen Mönchtum*, 144.
42. One is reminded of the manner in which the return of Odysseus to Ithaca takes place as a series of encounters with different, subhuman or suprahuman regimes of eating, against which Odysseus defines himself as human: see P. Vidal-Naquet, "Valeurs religieuses et mythiques." See now Schulz-Flügel, *Amator Eremi*, 220–25.
43. Rufinus, *Historia monachorum* 12.15.82, Festugière, 97; Schulz-Flügel, 330.

44. *Historia monachorum* 10.21–22.135–40, Festugière, 84. This is not in-cluded in the Latin translation: see Moschos, *Eschatologie*, 145, 174–78.

45. *Historia monachorum* 8.40.251–60, Festugière, 63–64; Schulz-Flügel, 299.

46. *Historia monachorum* 8.44.273–79, Festugière, 63–64; Schulz-Flügel, 300. One should note that Hermopolis was a pilgrimage site, connected with the visit of Christ to Egypt. Pilgrims may have brought to the monks wealth and food from outside.

47. *Historia monachorum* 1.46.296–58.383, Festugière, 27–32; Schulz-Flügel, 268–72.

48. Bagnall, *Egypt in Late Antiquity*, 283–84.

49. Bagnall, *Egypt in Late Antiquity*, 137.

50. Brown, *Authority and the Sacred*, 62–63.

51. Wipszycka, "L'attività caritativa dei vescovi egiziani." On the impressive furnishings of some of the churches in Egypt, see Wipszycka, "Church Treasures in Byzantine Egypt."

52. *Apophthegmata Patrum*, John Kolobos 41, in Guy, *Les Apophtegmes des Pères du Désert*, 130.

53. Georgi, *Remembering the Poor*, 84–92.

54. Till, *Koptische Heiligen- und Märtyrerlegende*, Coptic, 11; trans., 14.

55. Till, *Koptische Heiligen- und Märtyrerlegende*, Coptic, 17; trans., 23.

56. Giorda, *Monachesimo e istituzioni ecclesiastiche*, 20–23, 63.

57. *Apophthegmata Patrum*, Agatho 26: 116C.

58. Shenoute of Atripe, Letters 31 and 34, ed. Leipold and Crum, 95, 104. See Brown, *Power and Persuasion*, 155–56; and *Poverty and Leadership in the Later Roman Empire*, 101.

59. Dunand, "Between Tradition and Innovation." In a forthcoming cri-tique of the notion of the continuity of specifically Egyptian features in Coptic Christianity, Ariel López points out that mummification in the strict sense was not continued by Christians at this time.

60. Baumeister, *Martyr Invictus*.

61. Pseudo-Athanasius, *De anima et corpore* 8.1, ed. Budge, *Coptic Homilies*; trans. Bumazhnov, *Der Mensch als Gottes Bild*, 114.

62. Bumazhnov, *Der Mensch als Gottes Bild*, 81–108; Patterson, *Visions of Christ*.

63. *Bohairic Life of Pachomius* 100, trans. Veilleux, *Pachomian Koinonia* 1:137.

Conclusion

1. Patlagean, *Pauvreté économique et pauvreté sociale*, 130. For recent appre-ciations of the work of Évelyne Patlagean, see Flusin, "Récit de sain-teté"; and Freu, "Les pauvres en société."

2. John Rufus, *Plerophoriae* 88, *Patrologia Orientalis* 8:143.

3. Gaddis, *There Is No Crime*, 236–41.

4. Wipszycka, *Moines et communautés monastiques*, 401, commenting on Caner.

5. O'Malley, *Trent*, 248–75. (I owe this reference to the kindness of my friend Moshe Sluhovsky.)

6. Schachner, "Economic Production in the Monasteries," 63–68. The results of this brilliant survey have been condensed in a fundamental article: "The Archaeology of the Stylite."

7. Escolan, *Monachisme et Église*, 184; Brenk, "Monasteries as Rural Settlements." See now Schachner, "The Archaeology of the Stylite," 365, who finds no evidence for production in these sites.

8. Schachner, "The Archaeology of the Stylite," 378; Escolan, *Monachisme et Église*, 200–203, 253.

9. See, e.g., Theodoret of Cyrrhus on the monastery of Theodore at Rhôsos: "One could have seen some making sails, others hair coats, some plaiting mats and creels, others assigned to agriculture." *Historia religiosa* 10.3, trans. Price, 90. But we should note that Rhôsos was a coastal monastery, cut off from the Syrian hinterland by the steep southern end of the Amanus Mountains and so wide open to sea-borne Egyptian influences.

10. *A Letter of Philoxenus of Mabbug*, 14–15, ed. Olinder, 10*. I am particularly grateful to Professor David Michelson for having pointed out that this treatise has now been ascribed to Joseph Hazzaya (a Syriac author of the eighth century): Michelson, "A Bibliographic Clavis."

11. *A Letter of Philoxenus of Mabbug*, 24–25, p. 18*.

12. *The Discourses of Philoxenos of Mabbug*, trans. Kitchen, li.

13. Patlagean, *Pauvreté économique et pauvreté sociale*, 326; Bagnall, *Egypt in Late Antiquity*, 289—a landscape "recast" by Christian building. We know most about such building in Syria and Palestine: see Baumann, *Spätantike Stifter im Heiligen Land*; and Haensch, "Le financement de la construction." For Egypt, see now Grossmann, "Early Christian Architecture in Egypt."

14. Wipszycka, "Le fonctionnment intérieur des monastères," 182.

15. Caner, "Towards a Miraculous Economy."

16. López, *Shenoute of Atripe*, 46–72.

17. López, *Shenoute of Atripe*, 48.

18. López, *Shenoute of Atripe*, 50.

19. López, *Shenoute of Atripe*, 66.

20. Besa, *Life of Shenoute* 138–39, trans. Bell, 88–81. Whether this can now be called a *Life* of Shenoute by Besa is uncertain: see Lubomierski, *Die Vita Sinuthii*, 135–37.

21. Besa, *Life of Shenoute* 143, trans. Bell, 82.

22. Besa, *Life of Shenoute* 138, trans. Bell, 81.

23. For this immense theme, one can do no better than read the consecutive

volumes of Adalbert de Vogüé's *Histoire littéraire du mouvement monastique* (1991–).

24. Silber, *Virtuosity, Charisma and Social Order.*
25. Fa-hsien, *A Record of the Buddhistic Kingdoms,* 16; trans. Legge, 42.
26. Plotinus, *Enneads* 2.9.9: "Against the Gnostics," Armstrong, 2:256.
27. Gibbon, *Decline and Fall of the Roman Empire,* chap. 37, 2:352.
28. *Discourse on the Compassion of God and of the Archangel Michael,* trans. Budge, *Coptic Texts in the Dialect of Upper Egypt,* 757–58.

Bibliography

Alexander of Lycopolis. *An Alexandrian Platonist against Dualism: Alexander of Lycopolis' Treatise "Critique of the Doctrines of Manichaeus."* Trans. P. W. van der Horst and J. Mansfeld. Leiden: Brill, 1974.

Allberry, C. R. C., ed. *A Manichaean Psalmbook*, Part 2: *Manichaean Manuscripts in the Chester Beatty Collection.* Stuttgart: Kohlhammer, 1938.

Alster, B. *Proverbs of Ancient Sumer: The World's Earliest Proverb Collections.* Bethesda, Md.: CDL Press, 1998.

Amélineau, E. *Monuments pour servir à l'histoire de l'Égypte chrétienne au ivᵉ siècle: Histoire de saint Pakhôme et de ses communautés.* Paris: E. Leroux, 1887.

Anderson, G. A. *Charity: The Place of the Poor in the Biblical Tradition.* New Haven: Yale University Press, 2013.

Apostolic Constitutions. See Metzger.

Das Archiv des Nepheros und verwandte Texte. Ed. B. Kramer and J. C. Shelton. Aegyptiaca Treverensia 4. Mainz: P. von Zabern, 1987.

Assmann, J. *Death and Salvation in Ancient Egypt.* Ithaca: Cornell University Press, 2005.

Athanasius. *Life of Anthony.* Ed. G. J. M. Bartelink. Sources chrétiennes 400. Paris: Le Cerf, 1994. Trans. T. Vivian and A. A. Athanassakis as *The Life of Anthony: The Coptic Life and the Greek Life*, Cistercian Studies 209 (Kalamazoo, Mich.: Cistercian Publications, 2003).

Austin, M. M., and P. Vidal-Naquet. *Economic and Social History of Ancient Greece.* Berkeley: University of California Press, 1977.

Bagnall, R. S. *Egypt in Late Antiquity.* Princeton: Princeton University Press, 1993.

———, ed. *Egypt in the Byzantine World, 300–700.* Cambridge: Cambridge University Press, 2007.

———, ed. *The Kellis Agricultural Account Books.* Oxford: Oxbow, 1997.

———. "Monks and Property: Rhetoric, Law and Patronage in the *Apophthegmata Patrum*." *Greek, Roman and Byzantine Studies* 42 (2001): 7–24. Reprinted in Bagnall, *Hellenistic and Roman Egypt: Sources and Approaches.* Variorum Collected Studies. Aldershot, Hampshire: Ashgate, 2006.

Bailey, G., and I. Mabbett. *The Sociology of Early Buddhism*. Cambridge: Cambridge University Press, 2003.

Banaji, J. "Aristocracies, Peasantries and the Framing of the Early Middle Ages." *Journal of Agrarian Change* 9 (2009): 59–91.

Barclay, J. M. G. "Money and Meetings: Group Formation among Diaspora Jews and Early Christians." In *Vereine, Synagogen und Gemeinde im kaiserzeitlichen Kleinasien*, ed. A. Gutsfeld and D.-A. Koch, 113–27. Studien und Texte zu Antike und Christentum 25. Tübingen: Mohr Siebeck, 2006.

Baumann, P. *Spätantike Stifter im Heiligen Land: Darstellungen und Inschriften in Kirchen, Synagogen und Privathäusern*. Wiesbaden: Reichert, 1999.

Baumeister, T. *Martyr Invictus: Der Martyrer als Sinnbild der Erlösung in der Legende und dem Kult der frühen koptischen Kirche: Zur Kontinuität des ägyptischen Denkens*. Münster: Regensberg, 1972.

Beck, R. "Ritual, Myth, Doctrine and Initiation in the Mysteries of Mithras: New Evidence from a Cult Vessel." *Journal of Roman Studies* 90 (2000): 145–80.

BeDuhn, J. D. *Augustine's Manichaean Dilemma, 1: Conversion and Apostasy, 373–388 CE*. Philadelphia: University of Pennsylvania Press, 2010.

———. *The Manichaean Body: In Discipline and Ritual*. Baltimore: Johns Hopkins University Press, 2000.

———. "The Metabolism of Salvation: Manichaean Concepts of Human Physiology." In *The Light and the Darkness: Studies in Manichaeism and Its World*, ed. P. Mirecki and J. D. BeDuhn, 5–37. Leiden: Brill, 2001.

BeDuhn, J. D., and G. Harrison. "The Tebessa Codex: A Manichaean Treatise on Biblical Exegesis and Church Order." In Mirecki and BeDuhn, *Emerging from Darkness*, 33–87.

Bell, H. I. *Jews and Christians in Egypt*. London: British Museum, 1924.

Besa. *Life of Shenoute*. Trans. D. N. Bell. Cistercian Studies 73. Kalamazoo, Mich.: Cistercian Publications, 1983.

Bowersock, G. W. *Hellenism in Late Antiquity*. Ann Arbor: University of Michigan Press, 1990.

———. "Old and New Rome in the Late Antique Near East." In *Transformations of Late Antiquity: Essays for Peter Brown*, ed. P. Rousseau and M. Papoutsakis, 37–49. Farnham, Surrey: Ashgate, 2009.

Brakke, D. *Athanasius and the Politics of Asceticism*. Oxford: Clarendon Press, 1995.

Brenk, B. "Monasteries as Rural Settlements: Patron-Dependence or Self-Sufficiency?" In *Recent Research in the Late Antique Countryside*, ed. W. Bowden, L. Lavan, and C. Machado, 447–75. Late Antique Archaeology 2. Leiden: Brill, 2004.

Brian-Baker, N. J. *Manichaeism: An Ancient Faith Rediscovered*. Edinburgh: T. and T. Clark, 2011.

Brock, S. "Early Syrian Asceticism." *Numen* 20 (1973): 1–9. Reprinted in Brock, *Syriac Perspectives on Late Antiquity.* London: Variorum, 1984.

Brown, P. "Alms and the Afterlife: A Manichaean View of an Early Christian Practice." In *East and West: Essays in Ancient History Presented to Glen W. Bowersock*, ed. T. C. Brennan and H. I. Flower, 145–58. Cambridge, Mass.: Department of Classics, Harvard University, 2008.

———. *Augustine of Hippo: A Biography.* New Edition with an Epilogue. Berkeley: University of California Press, 2000.

———. *Authority and the Sacred: Aspects of the Christianization of the Roman World.* Cambridge: Cambridge University Press, 1995.

———. *The Body and Society: Men, Women and Sexual Renunciation in Early Christianity.* Twentieth Anniversary Edition. New York: Columbia University Press, 2008.

———. "The Diffusion of Manichaeism in the Roman Empire." *Journal of Roman Studies* 59 (1969): 92–103. Also in *Religion and Society.*

———. *Poverty and Leadership in the Later Roman Empire.* Menahem Stern Jerusalem Lectures. Hanover, N.H.: University Press of New England, 2002.

———. *Power and Persuasion in Late Antiquity: Towards a Christian Empire.* Madison: University of Wisconsin Press, 1992.

———. *The Ransom of the Soul: Wealth and the Afterlife in Early Western Christianity.* Cambridge, Mass.: Harvard University Press, 2015.

———. *Religion and Society in the Age of Saint Augustine.* London: Faber, 1972.

———. "The Rise and Function of the Holy Man in Late Antiquity." *Journal of Roman Studies* 61 (1971): 80–101. Reprinted in *Society and the Holy in Late Antiquity*, 103–52. Berkeley: University of California Press, 1982. Citations are to the Berkeley edition.

———. *The Rise of Western Christendom: Triumph and Diversity, AD 200–1000.* Tenth Anniversary Revised Edition. Oxford and Malden, Mass.: Wiley-Blackwell, 2013.

———. *Through the Eye of a Needle: Wealth, the Fall of Rome, and the Making of Christianity in the West, 350–550 AD.* Princeton: Princeton University Press, 2012.

———. "Treasure in Heaven: The Implications of an Image." *Cristianesimo nella storia* 33 (2012): 377–96.

Brunt, P. "Aspects of the Social Thought of Dio Chrysostom and the Stoics." *Proceedings of the Cambridge Philological Society* 19 (1973): 9–34.

Budge, E. A. W. *Coptic Homilies in the Dialect of Upper Egypt.* London: British Museum, 1910.

———. *Coptic Texts in the Dialect of Upper Egypt.* London: British Museum, 1915.

Buell, D. Kimber. "'Be Not One Who Stretches Out Hands to Receive and

Shuts Them When It Comes to Giving': Envisioning Charity When Both Donor and Recipient Are Poor." In *Wealth and Poverty in Early Church and Society*, 37–47. Holy Cross Studies in Patristic Theology and History. Grand Rapids, Mich.: Baker Academic, 2006.

Bumazhnov, D. *Der Mensch als Gottes Bild im christlichen Ägypten*. Studien und Texte zu Antike und Christentum 34. Tübingen: Mohr Siebeck, 2006.

———. *"Monakhos esti . . .": Mia ereuna stis aparkhes tou horou* ["He is a monk . . .": An investigation of the origin of the term]. Thira, Greece: Thesbitis, 2012.

Burghart, R. "Renunciation in the Religious Traditions of South Asia." *Man* 18 (1983): 635–53.

Burkitt, F. *Early Christianity outside the Roman Empire*. Cambridge: Cambridge University Press, 1899.

Butler, H. C. *Publications of the Princeton University Archaeological Expedition to Syria in 1904–5 and 1909*. Division 3, Greek and Latin Inscriptions, section B: Northern Syria, ed. W. K. Prentice. Leiden: Brill, 1922.

Cameron, A. *Christianity and the Rhetoric of Empire: The Development of Christian Discourse*. Berkeley: University of California Press, 1991.

Caner, D. "Towards a Miraculous Economy: Christian Gifts and Material 'Blessings' in Late Antiquity." *Journal of Early Christian Studies* 14 (2006): 329–77.

———. *Wandering, Begging Monks: Spiritual Authority and the Promotion of Monasticism in Late Antiquity*. Berkeley: University of California Press, 2002.

Carrié, J.-M., and A. Rousselle. *L'empire romain en mutation des Sévères à Constantin, 192–337*. Paris: Le Seuil, 1999.

Caseau, B. "L'image du mauvais moine: Les remnuoths et les sarabaïtes de Jérôme et Cassien." *Zbornik Radova Vizantinoloshkog Instituta* 46 (2009): 11–25.

Cassian, John. *Institutions cénobitiques*. Ed. and trans. J.-C. Guy. Sources chrétiennes 109. Paris: Le Cerf, 1965.

Cauvin, J. *The Birth of the Gods and the Origins of Agriculture*. Cambridge: Cambridge University Press, 2000.

Černý, J. *Coptic Etymological Dictionary*. Cambridge: Cambridge University Press, 1976.

Chaîne, M. "La double recension de l'Histoire Lausiaque dans la version copte." *Revue de l'Orient chrétien* 25 (1925): 232–75.

Chavannes, A., and P. Pelliot. "Un traité manichéen retrouvé en Chine." *Journal asiatique*, sér. 10, 18 (1911): 115.

Chenu, M.-D. *La théologie au douzième siècle*. Paris: Vrin, 1967. Trans. J. Taylor and L. K. Little as *Nature, Man, and Society in the Twelfth Century* (Chicago: University of Chicago Press, 1968).

Choat, M. "Property Ownership and Tax Payment in Fourth-Century Monasticism." In *Monastic Estates in Late Antique and Early Islamic Egypt: Ostraca, Papyri and Studies in Honour of Sarah Clackson*, ed. A. Boudhors, J. Clackson, C. Louis, and P. Sijpesteijn, 129–40. Oxford: Oxbow, 2009.

Cologne Mani Codex, The: Concerning the Origin of His Body. Trans. R. Cameron and A. J. Dewey. Missoula, Mont.: Scholars Press, 1979.

Coptic Documentary Texts from Kellis. Vol. 1, ed. I. Gardner, A. Alcock, and W. P. Funk. Oxford: Oxbow, 1999.

Cramer, W. *Die Engelvorstellungen bei Ephräm dem Syrer.* Orientalia Christiana Analecta 173. Rome: Vatican, 1965.

Crone, P. *The Nativist Prophets of Early Islamic Iran: Rural Revolt and Local Zoroastrianism.* Cambridge: Cambridge University Press, 2012.

Cyprian. *The Letters of Saint Cyprian of Carthage.* Trans. G. W. Clarke. Ancient Christian Writers 43–44, 46–47. New York: Newman Press, 1984–.

———. *Opera omnia.* Ed. W. Hartel. Corpus Scriptorum Ecclesiasticorum Latinorum 3:2. Vienna: Gerold, 1871.

Daley, B. *The Hope of the Early Church: A Handbook of Patristic Eschatology.* Cambridge: Cambridge University Press, 1991; 2nd ed., Grand Rapids, Mich.: Eerdmans, 2010.

Daloz, L. *Le travail selon Jean Chrysostome.* Paris: Lethielleux, 1959.

Decker, M. *"Tilling the Hateful Earth": Agricultural Production and Trade in the Late Antique East.* Oxford Studies in Byzantium. Oxford: Oxford University Press, 2009.

Desmond, W. D. *The Greek Praise of Poverty: Origins of Ancient Cynicism.* Notre Dame: Notre Dame University Press, 2006.

Diamond, E. *Holy Men and Hunger Artists: Fasting and Asceticism in Rabbinic Culture.* Oxford: Oxford University Press, 2004.

Didascalia Apostolorum, The: An English Version. Ed. A. Stewart-Sykes. Turnhout: Brepols, 2009.

Dijkstra, J., and M. van Dijk. *The Encroaching Desert: Egyptian Hagiography and the Medieval West.* Leiden: Brill, 2006.

Doctrine des Douze Apôtres, La: Didachè. Ed. and trans. W. Rofdorf and A. Tuiler. Sources chrétiennes 248. Paris: Le Cerf, 1978.

Dodds, E. R. *Pagans and Christians in an Age of Anxiety.* Cambridge: Cambridge University Press, 1965.

Doukellis, P. N. *Libanios et la terre: Discours et idéologie politique.* Bibliothèque archéologique et historique 145. Beirut: Institut Français d'Archéologie du Proche-Orient, 1995.

Downs, D. J. *The Offering of the Gentiles: Paul's Collection for Jerusalem in Its Chronological, Cultural and Cultic Context.* Tübingen: Mohr Siebeck, 2008.

Dunand, F. "Between Tradition and Innovation: Egyptian Funerary Practices in Late Antiquity." In Bagnall, *Egypt in the Byzantine World*, 163–84.

Duncan-Jones, R. *The Economy of the Roman Empire.* Cambridge: Cambridge University Press, 1974.

Duval, Y. *Chrétiens d'Afrique à l'aube de la paix constantinienne*. Paris: Institut des Études Augustiniennes, 2000.

Elm, S. Introduction to "Charisma and Society: The 25th Anniversary of Peter Brown's Analysis of the Late Antique Holy Man." *Journal of Early Christian Studies* 6 (1998): 343–52.

Escolan, P. *Monachisme et Église: Le monachisme syrien du ive au viie siècle: Un ministère charismatique*. Théologie historique 105. Paris: Beauchesne, 1999.

Fa-hsien. *A Record of the Buddhistic Kingdoms*. Trans. J. Legge. Oxford: Clarendon Press, 1886.

Fentress, J., and C. Wickham. *Social Memory*. Oxford: Blackwell, 1992.

Finley, M. I. *The Ancient Economy*. Berkeley: University of California Press, 1973.

Finn, R. *Almsgiving in the Later Roman Empire: Christian Promotion and Practice, 313–450*. Oxford: Oxford University Press, 2006.

Fitschen, K. *Messalianismus und Anti-messalianismus: Ein Beispiel ostkirchlicher Ketzergeschichte*. Forschungen zur Kirche- und Dogmengeschichte 71. Göttingen: Vandenhoek and Ruprecht, 1998.

Fleming, F. "Columbus as a Scriptural Exegete." In *Biblical Hermeneutics in Historical Perspective: Studies in Honor of Karlfried Froehlich on His Sixtieth Birthday*, ed. M. S. Burrows and P. Rorem, 173–83. Grand Rapids, Mich.: Eerdmans, 1991.

Flusin, B. "Récit de sainteté, famille et société: Évelyne Patlagean et l'hagiographie." In *Les réseaux familiaux: Antiquité tardive et moyen âge*, ed. Béatrice Caseau, 113–24. Centre de Recherche d'Histoire et Civilisation de Byzance, Monographies 37. Paris: Association des Amis du Centre, 2012.

Foster, B. R. *Before the Muses: An Anthology of Akkadian Literature*. Bethesda, Md.: CL Press, 2005.

Frank, G. *The Memory of the Eyes: Pilgrims to Living Saints in Christian Late Antiquity*. Berkeley: University of California Press, 2000.

Freu, C. *Les figures du pauvre dans les sources italiennes de l'antiquité tardive*. Paris: Boccard, 2007.

———. "Les pauvres en société à l'époque protobyzantine: Regards historiographiques sur l'oeuvre d'Évelyne Patlagean." In *Les réseaux familiaux: Antiquité tardive et moyen âge*, ed. Béatrice Caseau, 373–92. Centre de Recherche d'Histoire et Civilisation de Byzance, Monographies 37. Paris: Association des Amis du Centre, 2012.

Friesen, S. "Poverty in Pauline Studies: Beyond the So-Called New Consensus." *Journal for the Study of the New Testament* 26 (2004): 323–61.

Funk, W.-P. "The Reconstruction of the Manichaean *Kephalaia*." In Mirecki and BeDuhn, *Emerging from Darkness*, 143–59.

Gaddis, M. *There Is No Crime for Those Who Have Christ: Religious Violence in the Christian Roman Empire*. Berkeley: University of California Press, 2005.

Gardner, I., ed. *Kellis Literary Texts*. Oxford: Oxbow, 2007.

————. "Some Comments on Mani and Indian Religion according to the Coptic *Kephalaia*." In *Il Manicheismo: Nuove prospettive della ricerca*, ed. A. V. Tongerloo and L. Cirillo, 123–55. Turnhout: Brepols, 2005.

————. "'With a Pure Heart and a Truthful Tongue': The Recovery of the Text of the Manichaean Daily Prayer." *Journal of Late Antiquity* 4 (2011): 79–99.

Gardner, I., and S. N. C. Lieu. "From Narmouthis (Medinat Madi) to Kellis (Ismant al-Kharab)." *Journal of Roman Studies* 86 (1996): 146–69.

————, eds. *Manichaean Texts from the Roman Empire*. Cambridge: Cambridge University Press, 2004.

Gatz, B. *Goldene Zeit und sinnverwandte Vorstellungen*. Spudasmata 16. Hildesheim: Olms, 1967.

Georgi, D. *Remembering the Poor: The History of the Pauline Collection for Jerusalem*. Nashville: Abingdon Press, 1992.

Gibbon, E. *A History of the Decline and Fall of the Roman Empire*. New York: Random House, 1936.

Giorda, M. *Monachesimo e istituzioni ecclesiastiche in Egitto: Alcuni casi di interazione e di integrazione*. Bologna: Edizioni Dehoniane, 2012.

————. *Il regno di Dio in terra*. Rome: Edizioni di storia e letteratura, 2011.

Goehring, J. *Ascetics, Society, and the Desert: Studies in Early Egyptian Monasticism*. Harrisburg, Pa.: Trinity Press International, 1999.

————. "The Encroaching Desert: Literary Production and Monastic Space in Early Christian Egypt." *Journal of Early Christian Studies* 1 (1993): 281–96. Reprinted in *Ascetics, Society, and the Desert*, 73–88. Citations refer to journal publication.

————. "The World Engaged: The Social and Economic World of Early Egyptian Monasticism." In *Ascetics, Society and the Desert*, 39–52.

Gordon, R. "Individuality, Selfhood and Power in the Second Century: The Mystagogue as a Mediator of Religious Options." In *Religious Dimensions of the Self in the Second Century CE*, ed. J. Rüpke and G. Woolf, 146–72. Studien und Texte zu Antike und Christentum 76. Tübingen: Mohr Siebeck, 2013.

————. "Monotheism, Henotheism, Megatheism: Debating Pre-Constantinian Religious Change." *Journal of Roman Archaeology*, 27 (2014): 665–73.

Gould, M. "Recent Work on Monastic Origins." *Studia Patristica*, vol. 25, ed. E. A. Livingstone, 405–13. Louvain: Peeters, 1993.

Grafton, A., and M. Williams. *Christianity and the Transformation of the Book: Origen, Eusebius and the Library of Caesarea*. Cambridge, Mass.: Harvard University Press, 2006.

Griffith, S. "Images of Ephraem: The Syrian Holy Man and His Church." *Traditio* 45 (1989): 7–33.

Grossmann, P. "Early Christian Architecture in Egypt and Its Relationship to the Architecture of the Byzantine World." In Bagnall, *Egypt in the Byzantine World*, 103–36.

Guy, J.-C., ed. and trans. *Les Apophtegmes des Pères du Désert.* Etiolles, Essonne: Les Dominos, 1968.

Haensch, R. "Le financement de la construction des églises pendant l'Antiquité tardive et évergétisme antique." *Antiquité tardive* 14 (2006): 47–58.

Hamel, G. *Poverty and Charity in Roman Palestine.* Berkeley: University of California Press, 1990.

Harl, M. "La prise de conscience de la nudité d'Adam." In *Studia Patristica* 7, ed. F. L. Cross, 482–95. Texte und Untersuchungen 92. Berlin: Akademie Verlag, 1966.

Harvey, S. Ashbrook. "The Sense of a Stylite." *Vigiliae Christianae* 42 (1988): 376–94.

Heal, K. S., and R. A. Kitchen, eds. *Breaking the Mind: New Studies in the Syriac "Book of Steps."* Washington, D.C.: Catholic University of America Press, 2014.

Heiser, A. *Die Paulusinszenierung des Johannes Chrysostomus.* Studien und Texte zu Antike und Christentum 70. Tübingen: Mohr Siebeck, 2012.

Hermas. *Le Pasteur.* Ed. and trans. R. Joly. Sources chrétiennes 53 bis. Paris: Le Cerf, 1968.

Holman, S. *The Hungry Are Dying: Beggars and Bishops in Roman Cappadocia.* Oxford: Oxford University Press, 2001.

Hopkins, K. "Christian Number and Its Implications." *Journal of Early Christian Studies* 6 (1998): 185–226.

Horden, P., and N. Purcell. *The Corrupting Sea: A Study of Mediterranean History.* Oxford: Blackwell, 2000.

Irenaeus of Lyon. *Irénée de Lyon: Contre les hérésies.* Ed. A. Rousseau. Sources chrétiennes 100. Paris: Le Cerf, 1965.

James, W. *The Will to Believe and Other Essays in Popular Philosophy.* New York: Longmans, Green, 1896.

Johnson, S. F. *The Life and Miracles of Thekla: A Literary Study.* Cambridge, Mass.: Harvard University Press, 2006.

Judge, E. A. "The Earliest Use of Monachos for 'Monk' (P. Coll. Youtie 77) and the Origins of Monasticism." *Jahrbuch für Antike und Christentum* 20 (1977): 72–89.

Juhl, D. *Die Askese im Liber Graduum und bei Afrahat: Eine vergleichende Studie zur frühsyrischen Frömmigkeit.* Orientalia Biblica et Christiana. Wiesbaden: Harassowitz, 1996.

Julian, Emperor of Rome. *The Works of the Emperor Julian.* Ed. and trans. W. C. Wright. Loeb Classical Library. Cambridge, Mass.: Harvard University Press, 1953–59.

Kalmin, R. *The Sage in Jewish Society in Late Antiquity.* London: Routledge and Kegan Paul, 1999.

Koch, K. "Der Schatz im Himmel." In *Leben angesichts des Todes: Beiträge zum theologischen Problem des Todes: Helmut Thielicke zum 60. Geburtstag,* 47–60. Tübingen: Mohr, 1968.

Kofsky, A., and S. Ruzer. "Reading the Ascetic Ideal into Genesis 1–3: Hermeneutic Strategies in the *Book of Steps* Memra 21." In Heal and Kitchen, *Breaking the Mind,* 273–96.

König, J. "The Cynic and Christian Lives of Lucian's Peregrinus." In *The Limits of Ancient Biography,* ed. B. McGing and J. Mossman, 227–54. Swansea: The Classical Press of Wales, 2006.

Krauss, S. *Griechische und lateinische Lehnwörter in Talmud, Midrasch und Targum.* Berlin: S. Calvary, 1899.

Kretschmar, G. "Ein Beitrag zur Frage nach dem Ursprung frühchristlicher Askese." *Zeitschrift für Theologie und Kirche* 64 (1961): 27–67.

Kronholm, T. *Motifs from Genesis I–II in the Genuine Hymns of Ephraem the Syrian.* Lund: Gleerup, 1978.

Laniado, A. "The Early Byzantine State and the Christian Ideal of Poverty." In *Charity and Giving in Monotheistic Religions,* ed. M. Frenkel and Y. Lev, 15–43. Studien zur Geschichte und Kultur des islamischen Orients, neue Folge 22. Berlin: De Gruyter, 2009.

Lendon, J. *Empire of Honor: The Art of Government in the Roman World.* Oxford: Oxford University Press, 1997.

Lenski, N. "Valens and the Monks: Cudgeling and Conscription as a Means of Social Control." *Dumbarton Oaks Papers* 58 (2004): 93–117.

Levene, A. *The Early Syrian Fathers on Genesis.* London: Taylor's Foreign Press, 1951.

Leyser, C. "The Uses of the Desert in the Sixth-Century West." In Dijkstra and Dijk, *The Encroaching Desert,* 114–34.

Libanius. *Libanii Orationes.* Ed. R. Förster. Leipzig: Teubner, 1906.

———. *Selected Orations.* Vol. 2 of *Libanius: Selected Works.* Trans. A. F. Norman. Loeb Classical Library. Cambridge, Mass.: Harvard University Press, 1977.

Liber Graduum. Ed. M. Kmoskó. *Patrologia Syriaca* 3. Paris: Firmin-Didot, 1926.

——— Trans. R. Kitchen and M. F. G. Parmentier as *The Book of Steps: The Syriac Liber Graduum.* Cistercian Studies 195. Kalamazoo: Cistercian Publications, 2009. Kmoskó's text reprinted with a facing translation by Kitchen and Parmentier in *The Syriac Book of Steps,* fascicle 1 and fascicle 2 [*Memras* 1–10 and 11–20, respectively]. Texts from Christian Late Antiquity, 12 and 12b. Piscataway, N.J.: Gorgias Press, 2009–11.

Lieu, S. N. C. *Manichaeism in the Later Roman Empire and Medieval China.* 2nd ed. Tübingen: Mohr, 1992.

Lim, R. "Unity and Diversity among the Western Manichaeans: A Reconsideration of Mani's *sancta ecclesia.*" *Revue des études augustiniennes* 35 (1989): 231–50.

Lives of Simeon Stylites, The. Trans. R. Doran. Cistercian Studies 112. Kalamazoo, Mich.: Cistercian Publications, 1992.

Longenecker, B. "Exposing the Economic Middle: A Revised Economy

Scale for the Study of Early Urban Christianity." *Journal for the Study of the New Testament* 31 (2009): 243–78.

López, A. G. *Shenoute of Atripe and the Uses of Poverty: Rural Patronage, Religious Conflict, and Monasticism in Late Antiquity.* Berkeley: University of California Press, 2013.

Loraux, N. "*Ponos:* Sur quelques difficultés de la peine comme nom de travail." *Aiôn* 4 (1982): 171–92.

Lubomierski, N. *Die Vita Sinuthii.* Studien und Texte zu Antike und Christentum 45. Tübingen: Mohr Siebeck, 2007.

Lucian. *Lucian.* Ed. and trans. A. M. Harmon. 8 vols. Loeb Classical Library. Cambridge, Mass.: Harvard University Press, 1969.

Luijendijk, A. *Forbidden Oracles? The Gospel of the Lots of Mary.* Studien und Texte zu Antike und Christentum 89. Tübingen: Mohr Siebeck, 2014.

———. *"Greetings in the Lord": Early Christians and the Oxyrhynchus Papyri.* Harvard Theological Studies 60. Cambridge, Mass.: Harvard University Press, 2008.

Luomanen, P. "Where Did Another Rich Man Come From? The Jewish-Christian Profile of the Story about the Rich Man in the 'Gospel of the Hebrews.'" *Vigiliae Christianae* 57 (2003): 243–75.

Lutz, C. E. *Musonius Rufus: The "Roman Socrates."* Yale Classical Studies 10. New Haven: Yale University Press, 1942.

Macarius of Magnesia. *Macarios de Magnésie: Le Monogénès.* Ed. R. Goulet. Paris: Vrin, 2006.

Mani. *Kephalaia 1: Zweite Hälfte (Lieferung 13/14).* Ed. W.-P. Funk. Stuttgart: Kohlhammer, 1999.

Markschies, C. *Kaiserzeitliche christliche Theologie und ihre Institutionen.* Tübingen: Mohr Siebeck, 2007.

Meeks, W. *The First Urban Christians: The Social World of the Apostle Paul.* New Haven: Yale University Press, 1983.

Megitt, J. J. *Paul, Poverty and Survival.* Edinburgh: T. and T. Clark, 1998.

Metzger, M., ed. and trans. *Les constitutions apostoliques.* Sources chrétiennes 336. Paris: Le Cerf, 1987.

Michelson, D. "A Bibliographic Clavis to the Works of Philoxenos of Mabbûg." *Hugoye* 13 (2010): 279–344.

Millar, F. G. B. *A Greek Roman Empire: Power and Belief under Theodosius II.* Sather Classical Lectures 64. Berkeley: University of California Press, 2006.

Minnen, P. van. "Saving History? Egyptian Hagiography in Its Space and Time." In Dijkstra and Dijk, *The Encroaching Desert,* 57–91.

Mirecki, P., and J. BeDuhn, eds. *Emerging from Darkness: Studies in the Recovery of Manichaean Sources.* Nag Hammadi and Manichaean Studies 43. Leiden: Brill, 1997.

Morard, F. "Monachos, Moine: Histoire du terme grec jusqu'au 4e siècle: Influences bibliques et gnostiques." *Freiburger Zeitschrift für Philosophie und Theologie* 20 (1973): 332–411.

Moschos, D. *Eschatologie im ägyptischen Mönchtum.* Studien und Texte zu Antike und Christentum 59. Tübingen: Mohr Siebeck, 2010.

Murray, R. "The Exhortation to Candidates for Ascetical Vows at Baptism in the Ancient Syriac Church." *New Testament Studies* 21 (1974–75): 59–80.

Nedungatt, G. "The Covenanters of the Early Syriac-Speaking Church." *Orientalia Christiana Periodica* 39 (1973): 191–215, 419–44.

Niederwimmer, K. *The Didache: A Commentary.* Trans. L. M. Maloney. Ed. H. W. Attridge. Minneapolis: Fortress Press, 1998.

Nijf, O. M. van. *The Civic World of Professional Associations in the Roman East.* Amsterdam: J. C. Gieben, 1997.

North, J. D. "The Development of Religious Pluralism." In *Jews among Pagans and Christians,* ed. J. Lieu, J. North, and T. Rajak, 174–93. New York: Routledge, 1992.

O'Malley, J. W. *Trent: What Happened at the Council.* Cambridge, Mass.: Belknap Press of Harvard University Press, 2013.

Optatus. *Optatus: Against the Donatists.* Trans. and ed. M. Edwards. Liverpool: Liverpool University Press, 1997.

Origen. *Contra Celsum.* Trans. H. E. Chadwick. Cambridge: Cambridge University Press, 1965.

Osiek, C. *Rich and Poor in the Shepherd of Hermas: An Exegetical-Social Investigation.* Washington, D.C.: The Catholic Biblical Association of America, 1983.

Pachomius, Saint. *Instructions, Letters, and Other Writings of Saint Pachomius and His Disciples.* Trans. A. Veilleux. Vol. 3 of *Pachomian Koinonia.* Cistercian Studies 47 (1982).

———. *Pachomian Koinonia.* Trans. A. Veilleux. Cistercian Studies 45–. Kalamazoo, Mich.: Cistercian Studies, 1980–.

Palladius, Bishop of Aspuna. *Palladio: La Storia Lausiaca.* Ed. G. J. M. Bartelink. Rome: Mondadori, 1974.

———. *Palladius: The Lausiac History.* Trans. R. T. Meyer. Ancient Christian Writers 34. New York: Newman Press, 1964.

Papaconstantinou, A. *Le culte des saints en Égypte des Byzantins aux Abbasides.* Paris: CNRS, 2001.

Papyri Greek and Egyptian: In Honour of Eric Gardiner Turner. London: British Academy, 1981.

Patlagean, É. *Pauvreté économique et pauvreté sociale à Byzance: 4e–7e siècles.* Paris and The Hague: Mouton, 1977.

Patterson, P. A. *Visions of Christ: The Anthropomorphite Controversy of 399 CE.* Studien und Texte zu Antike und Christentum 68. Tübingen: Mohr Siebeck, 2012.

Pettipiece, T. *Pentadic Redaction of the Manichaean Kephalaia.* Leiden: Brill, 2009.

Philoxenus of Mabbug. *The Discourses of Philoxenos of Mabbug.* Trans. R. Kitchen. Cistercian Studies 235. Collegeville, Minn.: Liturgical Press, 2013.

————. *A Letter of Philoxenus of Mabbug Sent to a Friend.* Ed. G. Olinder. Acta Universitatis Gotoburgensis 1950:1. Göteborg: Elander, 1950.

Pietzner, K. *Bildung, Elite und Konkurrenz.* Studien und Texte zu Antike und Christentum 77. Tübingen: Mohr Siebeck, 2013.

Plotinus. *Plotinus.* Ed. and trans. A. H. Armstrong. Loeb Classical Library. Cambridge, Mass.: Harvard University Press, 1966.

Porphyry. *Porphyrius "Gegen die Christen," 15 Bücher. Zeugnisse, Fragmente und Referate.* Ed. A. von Harnack. Abhandlungen der preussischen Akademie der Wissenschaften 1916, philosophisch-historische Klasse. Berlin: Akademie der Wissenschaften, 1916.

Potter, D. *Constantine the Emperor.* Oxford: Oxford University Press, 2013.

Price, S. "Religious Mobility in the Roman Empire." *Journal of Roman Studies* 102 (2012): 1–19.

Rajak, T. "The 'Gifts of God' at Sardis." In *Jews in a Graeco-Roman World*, ed. M. Goodman, 229–39. Oxford: Oxford University Press, 1998.

Richter, S. G. *Die Heracleides-Psalmen.* Corpus Fontium Manichaeorum, Series Coptica 1: Part 2, fasc. 1. Turnhout: Brepols, 1998.

Rives, J. B. "Christian Expansion and Christian Ideology." In *The Spread of Christianity in the First Four Centuries: Essays in Explanation*, ed. W. V. Harris, 15–41. Leiden: Brill, 2005.

Rousseau, P. "Homily and Exegesis in the Patristic Age: Comparisons of Purpose and Effect." In *The Purpose of Rhetoric in Late Antiquity*, ed. A. L. Quiroga Puertas, 11–29. Studien und Texte zu Antike und Christentum 72. Tübingen: Mohr Siebeck, 2013.

Rubenson, S. *The Letters of Saint Anthony: Monasticism and the Making of a Saint.* Philadelphia: Fortress Press, 1995.

————. "Monasticism and the Philosophical Heritage." In *The Oxford Handbook of Late Antiquity*, ed. S. F. Johnson, 487–512. Oxford: Oxford University Press, 2012.

Rufinus of Aquileia. *Historia monachorum in Aegypto: Édition critique du texte grec.* Ed. A. J. Festugière. Subsidia Hagiographica 34. Brussels: Société des Bollandistes, 1961.

————. *Tyrannius Rufinus: Historia monachorum.* Ed. E. Schulz-Flügel. Patristische Texte und Studien 34. Berlin: De Gruyter, 1990.

Sahner, C. *Among the Ruins: Syria Past and Present.* London: Hurst and Company, 2014.

Sarris, P. *Economy and Society in the Age of Justinian.* Cambridge: Cambridge University Press, 2006.

Sayings of the Desert Fathers, The. Trans. B. Ward. Cistercian Studies 59. Kalamazoo, Mich.: Cistercian Publications, 1975.

Schachner, L. A. "The Archaeology of the Stylite." In *Religious Diversity in Late Antiquity*, ed. D. M. Gwynn and S. Bangert, 329–97. Late Antique Archaeology 6. Leiden: Brill, 2010.

————. "Economic Production in the Monasteries of Egypt and Oriens, AD 320–800." DPhil thesis, Oxford University, 2005.

Scheidel, W. "Stratification, Deprivation and Quality of Life." In *Poverty in the Roman World*, ed. M. Atkins and R. Osborne, 40–59. Cambridge: Cambridge University Press, 2006.

Schiavone, A. *The End of the Past: Ancient Rome and the Modern West.* Cambridge, Mass.: Harvard University Press, 2000.

Schöllgen, G. *Die Anfänge der Professionalisierung des Klerus und der kirchliche Amt in der syrischen Didaskalie.* Jahrbuch für Antike und Christentum, Ergänzungsband 26. Münster: Aschendorff, 1998.

————. *"Sportulae:* Zur Frühgeschichte des Unterhaltungsanspruch des Klerus." *Zeitschrift für Kirchengeschichte* 101 (1990): 1–20.

Schopen, G. *Buddhist Monks and Business Matters.* Honolulu: University of Hawaii Press, 2004.

Schulz-Flügel, E. *"Amator Eremi:* Zur Stellenwert des Begriffs 'Wüste' im ägyptischen und europäischen Mönchtum." In *Christliches Ägypten in der spätantiken Zeit*, ed. D. Bumazhnov, 217–29. Studien und Texte zu Antike und Christentum 79. Tübingen. Mohr Siebeck, 2013.

Schwartz, S. *Were the Jews a Mediterranean Society? Reciprocity and Solidarity in Ancient Judaism.* Princeton: Princeton University Press, 2010.

Scully, J. "Lowering in Order to Be Raised, Emptying in Order to Be Filled: The Ascetical System of the *Book of Steps.*" In Heal and Kitchen, *Breaking the Mind*, 297–312.

Shaw, B. D. *Bringing in the Sheaves: Economy and Metaphor in the Roman World.* Toronto: University of Toronto Press, 2013.

————. *Sacred Violence: African Christians and Sectarian Hatred in the Age of Augustine.* Cambridge: Cambridge University Press, 2011.

Shenoute of Atripe. *Sinuthii Archimandritae vita et opera omnia.* Ed. J. Leipoldt and W. E. Crum. Corpus Scriptorum Christianorum Orientalium 42, Shenoute Scriptores Coptici 2. Leipzig: Harassowitz, 1908.

Shils, E. *Center and Periphery: Essays in Macrosociology.* Chicago: University of Chicago Press, 1975.

Silber, I. *Virtuosity, Charisma and Social Order: A Comparative Study of Theravada Buddhism and Medieval Catholicism.* Cambridge: Cambridge University Press, 1995.

Skoyles, S. K. *Aphrahat the Persian Sage and the Temple of God: A Study of Early Syriac Theological Anthropology.* Piscataway, N.J.: Gorgias Press, 2008.

Slater, M. *William James on Ethics and Faith.* Cambridge: Cambridge University Press, 2009.

Smith, K. "Dendrites and Other Standers." *Hugoye* 12 (2009): 117–34.

————. "A Last Disciple of the Apostles: The 'Editor's' Preface, Rabbula's *Rules* and the Date of the *Book of Steps.*" In Heal and Kitchen, *Breaking the Mind*, 72–96.

Spickermann, W. "Philosophical Standards and Intellectual Life-Style: Lucian's Peregrinus-Proteus—Charlatan and Hero." In *Religious Dimensions of the Self in the Second Century CE*, ed. J. Rüpke and G. Woolf, 175–91. Studien und Texte zu Antike und Christentum 76. Tübingen: Mohr Siebeck, 2013.

Stein, M., ed. and trans. *Manichaica Latina*. Papyrologica Coloniensia 27/3:1. Paderborn: F. Schoningh, 2004.

Stewart, C. "By Way of a Preface." In Heal and Kitchen, *Breaking the Mind*, ix–xi.

———. *"Working the Earth of the Heart": The Messalian Controversy in History, Texts, and Language to AD 431*. Oxford: Clarendon Press, 1991.

Synesius of Cyrene. *The Essays and Hymns of Synesius of Cyrene*. Trans. A. Fitzgerald. Oxford: Oxford University Press; London: H. Milford, 1930.

———. *Synesii Cyrenensis Hymni et Opuscula*. Ed. N. Terzaghi. Rome: Regia Officina Polygraphica, 1944.

Talmud.

Babylonian Talmud. Ed. I. Epstein. Various translators. London: Soncino Press, 1935–48.

Pea/Ackerecke. Trans. G. A. Wewers. Übersetzung des Talmud Yerushalmi. Tübingen: Mohr Siebeck, 1986.

Le Talmud de Jérusalem. Trans. M. Schwab. Paris: Maisonneuve, 1972.

Tardieu, M. "La diffusion du bouddhisme dans l'empire kouchan, l'Iran et la Chine d'après un Kephalaion inédit." *Studia Iranica* 17 (1988): 153–82.

———. *Manichaeism*. Trans. M. B. de Bevoise. Urbana: University of Illinois Press, 2008.

Theissen, G. *The Social Setting of Pauline Christianity: Essays on Corinth*. Philadelphia: Fortress Press, 1982.

———. *Sociology of Early Palestinian Christianity*. Trans. J. Bowder. Philadelphia: Fortress Press, 1978.

Theodoret of Cyrrhus. *Historia religiosa*. Trans. R. M. Price as *A History of the Monks of Syria*, Cistercian Studies 88. Kalamazoo, Mich.: Cistercian Publications, 1985.

Thonemann, P. "Amphilochius of Iconium and Lycaonian Asceticism." *Journal of Roman Studies* 10 (2011): 185–205.

Till, W. *Koptische Heiligen- und Märtyrerlegende*. Orientalia Christiana Analecta 108. Rome: Pontificium Institutum Orientalium Studiorum, 1936.

Török, L. *Transfigurations of Hellenism: Aspects of Late Antique Art in Egypt, AD 250–700*. Probleme der Ägyptologie 23. Leiden: Brill, 2005.

Turner, P. *Truthfulness, Realism, Historicity: A Study of Late Antique Spiritual Literature*. Farnham, Surrey: Ashgate, 2012.

Ulrich, J. "What Do We Know about Justin's 'School' in Rome?" *Zeitschrift für Antikes Christentum* 16 (2012): 62–74.

Urbach, E. "Treasure Above." In *Hommage à Georges Vajda: Études d'histoire et pensée juives*, ed. G. Nahon and C. Touati, 117–24. Louvain: Peeters, 1980.

Vaggione, R. *Eunomius of Cyzicus and the Nicene Revolution*. Oxford: Oxford University Press, 2000.

Vaissière, E. de la. "Mani en Chine au vi^e siècle." *Journal asiatique* 292 (2005): 357–98.

Vandier, J. *La famine dans l'Égypte*. Cairo: Institut Français d'Archéologie Orientale, 1936. Reprint, New York: Arno, 1979.

Vidal-Naquet, P. "Valeurs religieuses et mythiques de la terre et du sacrifice dans l'Odyssée." *Annales E.S.C.* (Sept.–Oct. 1970): 1278–97. Reprinted in *Le chasseur noir*, 39–68. Paris: F. Maspero, 1981.

Vogüé, A. de. *Histoire littéraire du mouvement monastique, Première partie: Le monachisme latin*, 1. Paris: Le Cerf, 1991.

Ward-Perkins, J. B. "Frontiere politiche e frontiere cullturali." In *Persia e il mondo greco-romano*, 395–409. Accademia dei Lincei, anno 363, quaderno 76. Rome: Accademia dei Lincei, 1966.

West, M. L. *The East Face of Helicon: West Asiatic Elements in Greek Poetry and Myth*. Oxford: Clarendon Press, 1991.

Westerhoff, M. *Das Paulusverständnis im Liber Graduum*. Patristische Texte und Studien 64. Berlin: De Gruyter, 2008.

Will, P.-É. *Bureaucracy and Famine in Eighteenth-Century China*. Trans. Elborg Forster. Stanford: Stanford University Press, 1990.

Williams, M. S. *Authorized Lives in Early Christian Biography: Between Eusebius and Augustine*. Cambridge: Cambridge University Press, 2008.

Wipszycka, E. "*Anachôrités, erémités, enkleistos, apotaktikos:* Sur la terminologie monastique en Égypte." *Journal of Juristic Papyrology* 31 (2001): 147–68.

———. "Les aspects économiques de la vie de la communauté de Kellia." In *Le site monastique de Kellia*. Reprinted in *Études sur le christianisme dans l'Égypte de l'antiquité tardive*, 337–62. Studia Ephemeridis Augustinianum 52. Rome: Institutum Patristicum Augustinianum, 1996.

———. "L'attività caritativa dei vescovi egiziani." In *L'évêque dans la cité du ive au ve siècle: Image et autorité*, ed. É. Rebillard and C. Sotinel, 71–80. Collection de l'École Française de Rome 248. Rome: École Française de Rome, 1998.

———. "Church Treasures in Byzantine Egypt." *Journal of Juristic Papyrology* 34 (2004): 127–39.

———. "Contribution à l'étude de l'économie de la congrégation pachômienne." *Journal of Juristic Papyrology* 26 (1996): 167–210.

———. "Le fonctionnment intérieur des monastères et des laures en Égypte du point de vue de vie économique." *Journal of Juristic Papyrology* 31 (2001): 169–86.

———. "Les formes institutionnelles et les formes d'activité économique du monastère égyptien." In *Foundations of Power and Conflicts of Authority in Late Antique Monasticism*, ed. A. Camplani and S. Filoramo, 109–54. Orientalia Lovaniensia Analecta 157. Louvain: Peeters, 2007.

———. "The Institutional Church." In Bagnall, *Egypt in the Byzantine World*, 331–49.

———. *Moines et communautés monastiques en Égypte (ive–viiie siècles)*. Journal of Juristic Papyrology Supplements 11. Warsaw: Journal of Juristic Papyrology, 2009.

———. "Le monachisme égyptien et les villes." *Travaux et Mémoires* 12 (1994): 1–44.

———. "The Nag Hammadi Library and the Monks: A Papyrologist's View." *Journal of Juristic Papyrology* 30 (2000): 179–91.

———. "Quand a-t-on commencé à voir les moines comme un groupe à part?" *Journal of Juristic Papyrology* 27 (1997): 83–92.

Wischmeyer, O. *Die Kultur des Buches Jesus Sirach*. Berlin: De Gruyter, 1995.

Zanker, P. *The Mask of Socrates: The Image of the Intellectual in Antiquity*. Berkeley: University of California Press, 1995.

Zosimus. *Historia nova*. Trans. R. T. Ridley. Canberra: Australian Association for Byzantine Studies, 1982.

Index

Abbahu, Rabbi, 60
Acts 20:33–35, 10
Acts of Judas Thomas, 37
Adam and Eve: angelic labor in
  Eden, 59, 65, 73; fall of, xv, 52,
  56–60, 61, 66, 116–17; Jesus
  Christ as avatar of Adam, 60; lust
  for land of, 57, 59–60, 68; revers-
  ing fall of, 60. *See also* Eden
Against the Christians (Porphyry), 3
Agathon, Apa, 106
agyrtai, 41
aktémosyné, 83
Alexander of Lycopolis, 31
Alexander the Sleepless, 68
almsgiving. *See* charity (almsgiving)
Ambrosios, 33
amékhanôs, 102
Amélineau, Émile, 90
'amla. *See* drudgery (*ponos*)
Anderson, Gary, 6
angels: Adam and Eve's angelic
  labor, 59, 65, 73; angelic life of
  Symeon Stylites, 111; Egyptian
  monks as not, 98–99, 106, 108,
  117; as free from labor, 39, 59,
  61, 65, 70, 98, 103, 115; John the
  Dwarf of freedom from care of,
  81; Syrian holy men as living life
  of, 39, 60–61, 64, 70, 72, 75, 77,
  97, 103, 110, 114, 115, 116
anonymity, 25

Anthony, Saint, 75–78, 82, 87
Apollo, Apa, 102
Apollonius, Apa, 102
Apophthegmata Patrum (*Sayings of
  the Desert Fathers*), 80–81, 88,
  98, 111
apotaktikos, 71–72, 86
Artemidoros of Daldis, 22
ascetic movement: *Acts of Judas
  Thomas* written in, 37; Anthony
  chooses between forms of asceticism, 76; ascetics claim to be holy
  poor, 37, 72; Athanasius's *Life of
  Anthony* and, 77; divergent styles
  of ascetic life persist, 110–11;
  Franciscans and, 53; Manichaean
  movement seen as playing no
  role in, xxiv; Manichaeans as
  ascetics, 39; options narrowed
  in fifth and sixth centuries, 109;
  pagans on money and, 71; rise in
  non-Mediterranean regions, xix;
  Syrian versus Egyptian models,
  xxiv, 53, 70, 73, 77–78; on work,
  50. *See also* monasticism; Syrian
  radical Christian ascetics
Atargatis, sanctuary of, 41
Athanasius: on the Incarnation,
  106–7; *Life of Anthony*, 73, 76–78,
  82, 87, 88, 92; relationship with
  Egyptian monks, 76–77; on work
  of the hands, 94

Atrahasis myth, 51–52, 99

Augustine, Saint: as convert from Manichaeism, 79; on debate over monastic labor, 65; images of monasticism passed on by, 53, 115; issue of labor as peripheral for, 57; *On the Work of Monks* (*De opere monachorum*), 65, 79

autarky, 94–95

Bagnall, Roger, 74, 81, 86

Beck, Roger, 31–32

begging: *agyrtai*, 41; Apa Agathon's compassion for beggars, 106; Artemidoros of Daldis on Death as like, 22; Celsus on Jesus as beggar, 18–19; Egyptian monks did not beg, 53; holy poor compared with beggars, xii, xiv; Mani compares elect souls with beggars, 49; mendicant orders, 41, 53, 72; by radical movements of High Middle Ages, 115; Syrian ascetics who did not beg, 54

Benedict of Nursia, 53, 115

bishops: almsgiving centralized under, 24–27; charismatic monks versus institutional, 104, 109–10; church finances controlled by, 25–26; Egyptian monks' relations with neighboring, 103–6; episcopal elections, 27; as holy poor, xiii, 11, 36; as Levites, 36–37; monarchical episcopate, 25; remain poor in midst of wealth, 37; unitary episcopate, 29

body, the, 106–8

Bohairic [Coptic] Life of Pachomius, 108

Book of Steps, The, 57–60; on angelic labor of Adam, 59, 65; on care of the poor, 58–59, 73; on division between rich and poor, 61–62; on world as fallen, 68, 112, 116

bread, 47, 69, 100, 102, 103, 114

Buddhist monks, xxii, 41, 65, 115–16

Buell, Denise Kimber, 11

Bumazhnov, Dimitrij, 108

Burkitt, Francis, 55

Caner, Daniel, 52, 56, 112

Caribs, 120n5

Carrié, Jean-Michel, 30

Cassian, John, 53, 86, 88, 115

catechumens, 42, 45–46, 47, 48, 49

Cathars, 115

celibacy, 54, 72

Celsus, 18–19, 20

certainty, 33–34

charismatic-institutional conflict, 104, 109–10

charity (almsgiving): Anthony gives, 76; Anthony refuses, 76; *The Book of Steps* on, 58–59, 73; centralization of, 24–27; Christians as almsgivers, 46, 47; as countercultural, 22, 23; by Egyptian monks, 103–8; holy Christian wanderers of Syria supported by, 42; as inward looking in early Christianity, 21; Jesus on selling all one has and giving it to the poor, xi, 1, 2, 5, 36; as point of contact between believer and God, 6; reciprocity and, 21–24; sacralization of, 25; Syrian radical Christian ascetics on, 72–73

Christ. *See* Jesus Christ

Christianity: on angels, 60; charismatic-institutional conflict, 104, 109–10; church finances, 25–26, 112–14; Plotinus's criticism of, 117. *See also* ascetic movement; bishops; clergy; early Christianity; holy poor; Jesus Christ; Manichaean movement; monasticism

Eden: Adam and Eve's desire to own, 59; Adam and Eve's fall from, xv, 52, 58, 59; effortless abundance of, 52, 57, 60, 67; Egyptian monks visit, 102. *See also* Adam and Eve

Egypt: ascetic movement emerges in, xix; famine as concern in ancient, 100–101, 108; Joseph in, 100; laity of, 90–93; Manichaean movement in, 43–44, 70, 74–75; map of Greek East, *xx*; physicality as preoccupation of, 107; as reservoir of Christian thought and devotion, xxii–xxiii; sea route from Alexandria and Constantinople, 77; seeing as inter-visible with Syria, xxiii–xxv, 90; and social and religious ferment of Mediterranean and Fertile Crescent, 74–75; Syrian topography and climate contrasted with that of, 89–90; work as viewed in ancient, 99–101. *See also* Egyptian monks

Egyptian monks: access to holy provided to laity by, 92–93; agricultural work by, 84; *Apophthegmata Patrum* (*Sayings of the Desert Fathers*) on, 80–81, 88, 98, 111; Athanasius's *Life of Anthony* on, 73, 76–78, 82, 87, 88, 92, 94; authorized image of "true" monk, 73–81, 87; basketwork and plaiting done by, 84–85, 95, 99, 129n18; blending of Syrian model and, 111–12; the body as preoccupation of, 106–8; charity to the poor, 103–8, 117; the desert as represented by, 90; detachment from gifts received, 96; economic fragility of, 95, 128n18; engagement with real economy of Egypt, 85; as excep-

tional as seen from East, 116; *Historia Monachorum in Aegypto* on, 79, 101–3; image that the texts convey, 83–88; literature of, 87–88, 97; meaning of work for, 89–108; modern approaches to, 81–83, 90; as not angels, 98–99, 106, 108, 117; Palladius's *Lausiac History*, 73–74, 78, 82, 92, 94, 96–97; prayer to Archangel Michael, 118; property owned by, 86; reciprocal gift giving by, 97–98; relations with neighboring clergy, 103–6; residences of, 86; self-sufficiency of, 94–95, 96, 98; social and cultural diversity among, 87–88, 90; surplus created by, 85–86; Syrian holy men contrasted with, xxiv, 52–53, 70, 73, 77–78, 114–16, 117–18; work by, xxiv, 52–53, 70, 73–108, 116, 117, 118

Egypt in Late Antiquity (Bagnall), 74

Eirene, Lady, 44, 93, 94

Elijah, Prophet, 73

Elm, Susannah, 82

elm-and-vine parable, 7–8, 17, 22

empire romain en mutation des Sévères à Constantin, L' (Carrié and Rousselle), 30

Ephraem the Syrian, 55, 68

Epiphanius of Salamis, 78

equality of wealth, Paul on, 105–6

Escolan, Philippe, 52, 54, 56, 69

Eunomius, 14

famine, 100–101, 108

Faxian (Fa Hsien), 116

Fentress, James, 101

France, Anatole, 95

Francis, Saint, 72

Franciscans, 53, 64, 72, 115

Friesen, Steven, 7

Galatians 2:1–10, 9
Gardner, Iain, 44
Georgi, Dieter, 9
Gibbon, Edward, xvi, 117
Giorda, Mariachiara, 92, 106
giving: dangers of dependency-generating gifts, 23, 24, 33, 91, 94, 114; reciprocity in, 21–24; seen as zero-sum game, 113. *See also* charity (almsgiving); religious giving
Goehring, James, 77, 90
Gordon, Richard, 15
Grafton, Tony, 32
gratitude, 22, 23
Great Persecution, xix, 28
Greek East, xvi; decline of Western Roman Empire seen from, xvi–xvii; distinct society of, xvii–xviii; extent of, xxii; imperial system of, xvii; map, *xx–xxi*; Paul as biographical subject in, 79; Syrian versus Egyptian monastic models in, 53; as third world of ancient Christianity, xxii–xxiii. *See also* Egypt; Syria
"Greetings in the Lord": Early Christians and the Oxyrhynchus Papyri (Luijendijk), 32
Gregory of Nyssa, 14, 30

Habib of Amida, 68
heaven: joining earth and, 6, 17, 23, 35; yearning for touch of the divine on earth, 37–38. *See also* treasure in heaven
Hellé, Apa, 101
Heracleius, 71
Hermas, 7–8, 17, 22
Hesiod, xv, 52, 63
Hexapla (Origen), 33
Historia Monachorum in Aegypto (Rufinus of Aquileia), 79, 101–3

History of the Monks of Syria (Theodoret of Cyrrhus), 68
History Presented to Lausiac, The (Palladius). See *Lausiac History*
holy poor: ascetics as, 37, 72; bishops and clergy as, xiii, 11, 36; claim on pockets of the faithful, 34–35; defined, xii; *Didache* on claims of, 12; economic poor versus, 11, 35, 72, 106, 112; freedom from labor of, xv, 35; in Manichaean movement, 35, 46, 72; as mediators between average believers and God, xiv; membership of, 36; in monasteries and convents, xiii; numinous quality about them, xiv; Paul on dilemma of labor and, xii–xiii, xxii, xxiv, 1, 9–12, 17; proportions of wealth to go to real poor and, xv; should they work?, xix, xxii, 11, 65, 79–80, 111–12, 116; in spiritual exchange, xiv, 36; Syrian radical Christian ascetics as, 53; treasure in heaven in return for supporting, xiv; work issue brought to fore by, xiv–xv. *See also* monasticism; Syrian radical Christian ascetics
Hypatia, 98

Incarnation, the, 107
institutional-charismatic conflict, 104, 109–10
Isaac, 128n39

Jains, 41
James, William, 66
Jerome, Saint, 53, 78–79, 115
Jerusalem Talmud, 3
Jesus Christ: as avatar of Adam, 60; on brotherhood of Christians, 19; Celsus on him as religious entrepreneur, 18–19; defamil-

New History (Zosimus), 72
Nijf, Onno van, 27
North, John, 29
nuns. *See* monasticism

oikotypes, 101
On Dio and Life as Lived according to His Example (Synesius of Cyrene), 98–99
On the Work of Monks (De opere monachorum) (Augustine), 65, 79
ordo-building, 27–28, 103–4
Origen of Alexandria: on behavior of Christians of his time, 27; *Hexapla*, 33; on Jesus's challenge to Rich Young Man, 5; as monk-like scholar, 34; as teacher, 32–33, 87
orphans, 21
Oxyrhynchus papyri, 32

Pachomius, 83, 101, 108, 109, 128n37
pagans: Christian charity not extended to, 21; on Christian monks and money, 71, 72; on Christians murdering Hypatia, 98; and democratization of religious leadership, 13; Gregory of Nyssa compares Christianity with, 30; on Paul as religious entrepreneur, 10; Syrian holy men and, 41; on Syrian radical Christian ascetics, 64; on "treasure in heaven," 3–4
Palladius: first trip to Egypt, 78; *Lausiac History*, 73–74, 78, 82, 92, 94, 96–97; on work of the hands, 94
Pambo, Apa, 85, 96–97
Paphnutius, 92
Parmentier, Martien, 57
Patermuthius, 102
Patlagean, Évelyne, 109

patronage, 20, 23, 70, 90, 112–14
Patterson, Paul, 108
Paul, Saint: accusation that he was living off his followers, 10–11, 19, 114; appears to Shenoute in a vision, 114; as biographical subject, 79; on churches as organizations of the poor, 7; cited in debates over monastic labor, xix, 79–80; collection for poor of Jerusalem, xii, 1, 2, 9, 10, 17; on dilemma of labor and the holy poor, xii–xiii, xxii, xxiv, 1, 9–12, 17; on equality of wealth, 105–6; on food and clothing as sufficient, 83; as fund-raiser, 1, 9, 10, 20, 114; on giving surplus to the poor, 86; holy Christian wanderers of Syria compared with, 40; "If any will not work, let him not eat," xii, 80; letters of, 1, 9, 46, 79; Manichaean missionaries seen as avatars of, 43; Mani compares himself with, 42; as model for monks, 79–80; seen as religious entrepreneur, 10; speech at Miletus, 10; on spiritual exchange, xii, 9, 18, 36, 51; as worker, 10, 11, 15, 79–80
Pauvreté économique et pauvreté sociale à Byzance (Patlagean), 109
pax Byzantina, xvii
Peregrinus, 19, 20, 22, 38
philosophers, 94
Philoxenos of Mabbûg, 112
Plotinus, 3, 117
ponos. *See* drudgery (*ponos*)
poor, the: ancient Egyptian conception of, 100; Anthony's alms-giving to, 76; *The Book of Steps* on division between rich and, 61–62; bringing rich and poor together,

5–8, 17, 23; Christ's sufferings compared with those of, 107; deserving, xiii–xiv; economic versus holy, 11, 35, 72, 106, 112; Egyptian monks' charity to, 103–8, 117; Egyptian monks' poverty, 83; Franciscan poverty, 64, 72; Jesus on selling all one has and giving it to, xi, 1, 2, 5, 36; as local poor of Christian communities, 20–21; Manichaean Elect as, 42–43; Manichaean movement and real, 46, 49, 51; Mani on Blessed Poverty, 72; Paul collects for poor of Jerusalem, xii, 1, 2, 9, 10, 17; Paul on giving surplus to, 86; Plotinus on Christianity's undue concern with poverty, 117; poverty of holy Christian wanderers of Syria, 40; proportions of wealth to go to holy poor and real, xv; real poor as faceless, xiv; rich Christians expected to spend a portion of their wealth on, xi, 118; and rich seen as antithetical, 5, 6, 7; Syrian radical Christian ascetics on division between rich and, 61–62, 117. *See also* charity (almsgiving); holy poor

Porphyry, 3, 10

poverty. *See* poor, the

Poverty and Leadership (Brown), xi

prayer: by Adam and Eve in Eden, 59, 65, 73; *The Book of Steps* on that of the Perfect, 60; by Messalian monks, 58, 78; by monks and nuns, 11; wealth exchanged for, xiv, 8, 22–23, 24–25, 26–27, 45, 46, 93–94, 115

Prophecy of Neferti, 100

prophets, 11, 12, 19, 38

Psalm 78:19, 102

Questions of Theodore, 113

rabbis: code for giving to the poor, 23–24; on dangers of dependency-generating gifts, 23, 33, 91; on Monobazos, 3; in spiritual exchange with average Jews, 8, 17; systems of religious giving developed to support, 15–16; treatment of rich donors by, 24

Ransom of the Soul, The (Brown), xvi

reciprocity: charity and, 21–24, 91; by Egyptian monks, 97–98

regno di Dio in terra, Il (Giorda), 92

religion: zeal of second and third centuries, 29–35. *See also* Christianity; Judaism; pagans

religious entrepreneurs: image in second century AD, 17–20, 65; Paul seen as, 10

religious giving: Christian debates over, xvi, 11; Jesus on it being more blessed to give than to receive, 10; Jesus versus Paul on, 1–2; systems developed to support religious leaders, 15–16, 29. *See also* charity (almsgiving)

religious leaders: bishops and clergy as holy poor, xiii, 11; as closely monitored, 20; democratization of religious leadership, 12–16, 18; financial support of as charged issue, 10; paying for Christian, 11; seen as paying off, 14; systems of religious giving developed to support, 15–16, 29. *See also* bishops; clergy; rabbis

Remembering the Poor: The History of the Pauline Collection for Jerusalem (Georgi), 9

resurrection of the flesh, 107–8

rich, the: *The Book of Steps* on division between poor and, 61–62; bringing rich and poor together, 5–8, 17; expected to spend a portion of their wealth on the

rich, the (*continued*)
poor, xi, 118; and poor seen as antithetical, 5, 6, 7; Porphyry on them impoverishing themselves and becoming burden to others, 3; Syrian radical Christian ascetics on division between poor and, 61–62, 117. *See also* wealth
Robert, Louis, 63
Roman Empire: decline of Western, xvi–xvii; giving in, 21; intermediate layers of society, 31; religious zeal of second and third centuries, 29–35; social polarization in, 7, 31. *See also* Greek East
Romans: 15:14–32, 9; 15:26, xii, 1
Rousselle, Aline, 30
Rufinus of Aquileia, 79
Rule of Saint Benedict, 53, 115

Sahner, Christian, 39
sangha, 115
Sarris, Peter, 67
Sayings of the Desert Fathers (*Apophthegmata Patrum*), 80–81, 88, 98, 111
Schachner, Lukas, 111, 128n18
Scheidel, Walter, 31
Schöllgen, Georg, 24, 25
Schopen, Gregory, 87
Schwartz, Seth, 23, 37
Sennedjem, 99
Serinos, Apa, 95
sexual desire, 57, 59, 83
Shakespeare, William, 15
Shenoute of Atripe, 80, 107, 113–14
Shenoute of Atripe and the Uses of Poverty (López), 74, 113
Social Memory (Fentress and Wickham), 101
spiritual exchange: *The Book of Steps* on, 58–59; in Buddhism, 115; Cynic Demonax and, 38; with Egyptian monks, 97; emergence

in Christianity and Judaism, 8, 17; incommensurables joined in, 23; in Manichaean movement, 39, 46, 48, 51; Paul on, xii, 9, 18, 36, 51; prayer exchanged for wealth, xiv, 8, 22–23, 24–25, 26–27, 45, 46, 93–94, 115; with Syrian radical Christian ascetics, 65, 68–69
Stewart-Sykes, Alistair, 24
Stylite hermits: in fifth and sixth century Syria, 111. *See also* Symeon Stylites
Symeon Stylites: angelic life of, 111; on charity, 72–73; competitive holiness of, 56; in Greek East, xvii; individualism of, 55; in marginal zones, 67; perpetual rapt worship of, 60–61; in resolution of social grievances, 68; Shenoute of Atripe as contemporary, 80; work-free disciples of, 64
Synesius of Cyrene, 98–99
Syria, 39–40; *Acts of Judas Thomas* written in, 37; agricultural boom in, 62–64; ascetic movement emerges in, xix; bilingualism of, 40; as closer to Galilee of Jesus than was Mediterranean Christianity, 42; coastal plains versus hill villages of hinterland, 67–68; competitive holiness among monks, 56; cultural interchanges in, 39–40; *Didascalia Apostolorum* from, 24–25; drudgery (*ponos*) as viewed in, 52, 98; Egyptian topography and climate contrasted with that of, 89–90; geographic and cultural diversity of, 39; as grand junction linking Asia and the Mediterranean, 40; holy Christian wanderers of, 40–42; map of Greek East, xx–xxi; northern corridor of, 40; as res-

wealth (*continued*)
that it circulates properly and regularly within churches, 20; as freedom from labor, 13–14; Jesus and redistribution of, 5; keeping it so as to give constant aid to the poor, 27; Manichaean view of, 48, 49; monks and money, 71–73; new attitudes toward, 112–14; Paul on equality of, 105–6; philosophers could be trusted with money, 94; Plotinus on Christianity's undue concern with, 117; prayer exchanged for, xiv, 8, 22–23, 24–25, 26–27, 45, 46, 93–94, 115; proportions to go to holy poor and real poor, xv; provides leisure for religious activity, 13; renunciation of, 2, 9, 17, 25; traditions of Jesus and Paul on use of, 1–2; variations in Syria, 63. *See also* rich, the; treasure on earth

Weber, Max, 104, 109, 110

Were the Jews a Mediterranean Society? Reciprocity and Solidarity in Ancient Judaism (Schwartz), 23

West, Martin, 40

White Monastery, 113–14

Wickham, Chris, 101

widows, 21

Williams, Megan, 32

Williams, Michael, 80

Wipszycka, Ewa, 82, 86, 104–5, 128n18

Wisdom of Ben Sira/Ecclesiasticus, 14, 15

work (labor): by Adam and Eve in Eden, 59, 65, 68; Adam con-

demned to, 52, 56–60, 66, 117; angels as free from, 39, 59, 61, 65, 70, 98, 103, 115; by Anthony, 76; artistic depictions of labors of the months, 67; of dependent peasants, 68; by Egyptian monks, xxiv, 52–53, 70, 73–108, 116, 117, 118; Egyptian view of, 99–101; Greco-Roman ambiguity regarding, 66–68; of the hands, 10, 53, 76, 78, 84, 85, 94, 96, 98, 110, 117; holy poor as free from, xv, 35; holy poor bring issue to fore, xiv–xv; humanity defined by, xiv, 51–52, 57, 59, 67, 98, 99, 116; Manichaean Elect do not, 39, 48–49, 51; meaning of work for Egyptian monks, 89–108; by Paul, 10, 11, 15, 79–80; Paul's "If any will not work, let him not eat," xii, 80; by philosophers, 94; positive aspects of, 66–67; positive results of Syrian, 63–64; religious significance of, 66; seen as disqualifying one for intellectual pursuits, 14–15, 30, 66; should holy poor work?, xix, xxii, 11; should monks work?, xix, xxii, 11, 65, 79–80, 111–12, 116; Syrian view of, 99; wealth as freedom from, 13–14; work-free Syrian holy men, xxiv, 39, 50, 51–52, 53, 64–68, 70, 74, 79, 89, 103, 115. *See also* drudgery (*ponos*)

Works and Days (Hesiod), xv, 52, 63

Zanker, Paul, 34

Zosimus, 72